It's All About Me

The Best Life Anyone Could Have

BEING AN AUTOBIOGRAPHY OF

BEVERLY HEAD PICKUP ST. JOHN

2014
Cumberland Presbyterian Church
Cordova (Memphis), Tennessee

First Edition, First Printing, May 2014

ISBN-13: 978-0692200278
ISBN-10: 0692200274

Cumberland Presbyterian Church
8207 Traditional Place
Cordova (Memphis), Tennessee 38016-7414

It's All About Me

The Best Life Anyone Could Have

Contents

Beverly with big sister Eleanor

My Story

    My story actually begins in 1857 when my great-grandfather, George Pickup and his family came to America. George and his wife Martha arrived by boat with their baby girl, Mary Jane. They first settled in Massachusetts where they had been told were some textile mills. But being unable to find a job, they searched other possibilities and learned that there were some textile mills in Tennessee, far south from Massachusetts. So they moved to Shelbyville, Tennessee where George found work at the Sylvan Cotton Mills—an established mill. Unfortunately the mill burned soon after he moved there so George was forced to find another place for employment. Not too many miles away in Belvidere, Tennessee, Falls Mill was for sale. He knew a man who was interested in purchasing the mill, so they decided to become joint owners of Falls Mill. George was very excited because the mill was fed by two streams and he thought that there would be enough power to be able to make some plaid fabric like he had been able to make in England. Unfortunately it was not. Therefore, after a few years as the owner of Falls Mill, as beautiful as it was, he sold the property back to the original owner and retired to his farm where he lived for the rest of his life.

By that time his son George, who had attended Webb School in nearby Bell Buckle, wanted to start his own business in Shelbyville. He also wanted to marry a young lady whom he had met named Rebecca Cannon from Chattanooga, Tennessee. They married and had four children, Ernest, Ethel, Elbert, and Harry. The family continued to live in the Shelbyville area where George was honing his skills in the printing business, something that he did for the rest of his life.

George and Rebecca's first child, Ernest was born on April 10, 1887. When Ernest was twelve years old he was taken out of school to become an apprentice in the printing business with his father. During that period of time, without his father's knowledge he hid out in the attic of their home at night teaching himself to draw! He had always wanted to be a commercial artist but didn't want to disappoint his father. Finally, when he had some samples of his work to show, he started looking for some commercial work and, in 1912 he told his father that he was leaving the printing business to start his own business as an artist. His father responded "Well, son—I hope you do well, but if you don't make it, don't come to me looking for a job!" They were alienated for a year or so, but when "Pop" recognized that Ernest was succeeding, he and his father became friends again.

When Ernest was 25 he met and married Bessie James Wickware of Gallatin, Tennessee on June 18, 1912. Their first child, Eleanor Ann was born on December 26, 1915. I was born on October 14, 1918 near the end of World War I when a worldwide flu pandemic was raging. My father was quarantined at the Powder Plant in Old Hickory where he was working for the War effort. So he didn't see me until I was two weeks old. Fortunately the war was winding down and he was released from duty along with all of the men in uniform.

So…what else was going on in 1918?

- President Wilson was negotiating with the governments of Germany, Austria and Hungary for an armistice for World War I.
- People were talking the about the heroic efforts of Sgt. York who killed 25 Germans and captured 125.
- Mae West made her debut.
- And doctors everywhere were talking about the flu epidemic and the related dangers.

I could find nothing else of interest listed on my internet research for October 14th, 1918 so I suppose that my birth was the major event! At least it was for me!

I have a clipping about a reception given by the Gallatin Bar Association in honor of my grandmother, Eva Gammon and her husband, Jerry Wickware, a "rising Gallatin attorney." Dr. Beverly Head (for whom I was named) is acknowledged in the article as the late grandfather of the bride. We have a beautiful walnut candle stand in the living room that was made by him (I was told) when he was a prisoner during the Civil War—it is indeed one of my favorite treasures.

My parents, Bessie James Wickware, and Ernest Alexander Pickup, met at the Hobson Memorial Baptist Church in Nashville. The story goes that he sat behind Bessie one Sunday and later told his friends that he would "like to meet that young lady wearing a big black hat." That arrangement was made and the rest of the story is history!

My mother was 27 at the time of my birth, and a flu epidemic was attacking young adults all over the world. It was something of a miracle that she was not a victim of the scourge that claimed the lives of 600 million people over the world—one sixth of the world's population—and over 800,000 in the United States. So, I feel blessed to have been born at all! But blessings have followed me all of my life and this account will verify that fact. *Indeed—I had the best life that anyone could have!*

North 14th Street (East Nashville)

My parents, my sister Eleanor and I were living on Forest Avenue in East Nashville in 1918, but soon after my birth my grandmother (whom we called Maudie) came to live with us, followed by my mother's sister, Velma. It was obvious that they needed more room, so Daddy purchased a house on North 14th Street that had four bedrooms—enough to house our growing family. Unfortunately, my grandmother had been diagnosed with uterine cancer and life for her was fragile. Aunt Velma had gotten a job in Nashville with a real estate company and needed a place to live for a while. So with two little ones and four adults we had a good life there for five years.

The years on North 14th Street hold many wonderful memories for me. We had a wide front porch and a large backyard with peach trees, a big rope swing, and lots of space for play. We had a chicken coop and I remember Mother wringing a chicken's neck and watching it flop around until it died. She then dipped it into boiling water to loosen the feathers, and pick the feathers off, cut it up and fry the pieces in a skillet. Daddy always gave me the "pulley bone." I guess that it was called that because after I ate the meat off of the bone, Eleanor and I would pull it apart, and whoever got the largest piece of the bone could make a wish and it would come true! I also remember that my grandmother "Maudie" would sit in a chair and watch us while we played. Although my Aunt Velma was living with us, she went to work everyday so we didn't see much of her.

One day, at age four, I took a notion to venture out on my own, so I wrapped an orange in a towel, tied it to a long stick, put it over my shoulder and took off down the alley that led to Gallatin Road. That was a path that I knew quite well for it was the route that we took to the grocery store, the post office and the drugstore to get ice cream with Minnie, our twice a week housekeeper. I was walking happily along when suddenly my mother grabbed me by the arm and dragged me home—and fussing about my folly all of the way! (How well I remember!) I don't think that I ever considered leaving home again (until I got married of course)!

When Eleanor turned six she started to school, and she was ready! The story goes that she had been pre-registered, so Mother took her to school on her first day, left her at the front steps, and started home. When she looked back to make sure Eleanor had gone inside she saw her sit down on the steps, open her lunch, and start eating! Mother had to go back and take her hand and lead her into the school. Yes—she was ready all right—ready to eat her lunch out of her new lunchbox!

While we were living on North 14th Street we attended Eastland Baptist Church on Gallatin Road. I remember my Sunday school teacher was a sweet, plump woman with gray hair and a very soft lap. I loved for her to read us interesting stories about Jesus and his disciples and singing "Jesus Loves Me, this I Know."

Mother had a number of illnesses while we were there—the first was a miscarriage, followed by appendicitis. When I was four Mother developed a serious lung disease and had to have surgery. One rib was taken out in order to remove the infected lung. She was sent home to recuperate and the doctor came by every day, but Daddy hired a nurse to be with her most of the time. The doctor came so often that I thought that Mother was going to die—and she almost did. Daddy employed a young black woman named Minnie to take care of us during the day until he got home at night. One day Minnie was giving me a bath in a galvanized tub in a room by the kitchen. I asked Minnie if my mama was going to die. Her response is one that I will never forget: "Miss Beverly—yo' mama is an awful sick woman, and she could die. But she has a good doctor, and a nurse and your sweet daddy trying to get her well—but you need to learn right now that troubles is a part of livin.'" A few months into her recovery the doctor suggested that Daddy consider moving us out of Nashville "to the country" because the smog was so pervasive and he felt that Mother would have a better chance of recovery if we moved "where she could have more fresh air." Of course Daddy did what most any husband would do: he bought a car and engaged a real estate agent and started looking for some rural property.

We Move to Brentwood

How well I remember the day when we drove down a country road (Hill Road) in Brentwood—about eight miles south of downtown Nashville. Daddy stopped the car and we all got out and headed up a slope toward what looked like a house! The grass and weeds were so high that Daddy put me on his shoulder to make the trek up to what turned out to be a little two-room weathered shack. I listened to them talking about closing in the front porch to make a living room—giving us a three-room cabin in which to start our new life "in the country." I was excited—and they were too.

The next thing I knew, we were driving to "the country" every Saturday to see how the little house was looking! I thought it was beautiful! They also built a garage for "our new car" as well as a little "outhouse" that Mother named the "doodad." The day finally came when we were moving our furniture: a sofa and one chair for the living room and a small table with four chairs at the end of the living room for our "dining room." The bedroom had a three-quarter bed for Mom and Dad, and a cot for my sister and me—ages eight and five. The kitchen had an old iron wood stove with a flue attached to a small chimney, a little work table for making biscuits and a little cabinet. There was a screened door out the back that led to the "outhouse."

Eleanor was so excited to be starting to a new school—

9

Robertson Academy—a county school that was named for James Robertson, one of the founders of Nashville. It was an eight-grade public school and she began in the third grade. The building was a white framed building with stone steps leading up the large front door on a plot of about three acres. If Daddy didn't take her to school, she walked about four or five city blocks to a place where the Franklin-to-Nashville Interurban stopped to pick up passengers along Franklin Pike.

I was five so I stayed at home and played with Flash, my German Shepherd dog that Daddy purchased soon after we moved. I also had some rabbits to care for, and a wonderful playmate, Sue Perkins Craig who lived in a big log house back of us. Her aunt, Mrs. Ben Allen, with whom she lived, had a stile built over the fence so Sue and I could visit each other—as often as Mother would let me! Sue was only three and I was five—so I treated her like she was my little sister. I loved her dearly.

Mrs. Allen had a big Cadillac and a chauffeur who occasionally took Sue and me to get ice cream. The car had "jump seats" that folded down in the middle and that is where we chose to ride. One time Mrs. Allen took us to downtown Nashville where she had an apartment in the Polk Apartments, (named for President James K. Polk of Tennessee). The apartment is where she went to live in the wintertime when it was very cold and the big log house was hard to heat. Sue was a bit spoiled because Mrs. Allen gave her anything her little heart desired. Mother had to be very strict, not with me, but with Mrs. Allen because she thought that I ought to be allowed to "come and play with Sue" whenever she wanted me there. And I knew better than to beg!

Mother employed a man by the name of "Uncle" Joe Phillips to care for the lawn on a riding mower that we had. Because she called him "Uncle Joe" I thought that we were kin to each other. He would let me ride on the mower sitting in his lap. One day I asked him if he had any children. "Yes—I have a little girl about your age." I asked "can she come and play with me?" "If 'n yo' mama will let her, I will." So I ran and asked Mother if Joe's little girl could come and play with me and she said "that would be just fine." So the next day Uncle Joe brought Sissy with him. I noticed that she had a package wrapped in newspaper under her arm and I asked her what it was. "This is my lunch—I thought that we might eat lunch together." I was thrilled! So I ran into the house and asked Mother if she would fix me a lunch and wrap it up in newspaper. She smiled with understanding and agreed. I couldn't wait until time for lunch. So when Uncle Joe stopped to eat his lunch, Sissy and I sat down under a tree and ate our lunch. Then we found some rocks for furniture, some green moss for a rug and made us a little house and "pliked" (play liked) we had a little girl and a dog for us to play with. It was such fun! I was so happy to have another playmate during the summer when the grass needed cutting.

We soon discovered that there were lots of kids in the neighborhood: the Vaughns across the street had four children: an older sister Stella, and an older son, Billy Jim (who taught me how to play tennis), a girl Eleanor's age, Abby, and a boy a little older than me named Bobby. The Vaughns had a tennis court and a large front lawn for playing baseball. Next door to the Vaughn family was the Jackson family—they had four children too: Billy and Andrew about Eleanor's age, a boy my age named Clayton, and a younger sister Nancy. They didn't participate very much in the "gang" gatherings at our house, but we got together once in a while as we got older. Next door to the Jackson's was the Hopton family with two sons a little older than me, and a daughter named Vivian who was my age. They all went to a private school so we didn't have much in common with them except that Vivian had a pony and she and I rode together once in a while. Farther down Hill Road was the Morgan family whose oldest child was named Mary Virginia. She was between my sister and me and we got along very well. She had a brother, who was my age named Frank, and a younger brother Billy. Next door to the Morgans was Dake Gleaves—an only child who joined in the fun.

The boys in the neighborhood got together once in a while and one summer they dug out a 10x10 hole in the creek behind the Morgan's house and that provided us a place to enjoy trying to swim after a rain when the "creek was up." During the summer time we played outside at night—usually at our house: kick-the-can and hide-and-go-seek. We liked to skate together up and down Hill Road—especially on the level part. However, one time the boys decided to skate down the hill from Franklin Pike and when they did, they squatted down and rolled the rest of the way to the Vaughn's gate. So…I thought that I would try to do that, but I met my fate—when I squatted down I fell flat on my face and broke my two front teeth! I was about eleven years old and the whole episode made my mother very angry! It was because I had my permanent teeth—damaged pretty bad! But you know what? I didn't let my "snaggled teeth" smiles keep me from enjoying life to the fullest—at school or at play around the neighborhood! For me, it was just a part of growing up! Life was so exciting for me that "little things" like that didn't matter. In those days, we were expected to be neat and modestly dressed, but we didn't think much about looks like girls do now. I had some denim overalls and some "play clothes" that Mother made for me. I enjoyed watching her at the sewing machine—especially if she was making a dress for me!

Eleanor Has a
Life Changing Accident

One day my sister went across the road to have a visit with Abby Vaughn. But when she was running up the driveway she stumbled and fell. About that time a man came by in his car, saw her lying there and stopped to see if he could help her. He saw that her knee was out of joint so he picked her up and jerked her knee back into joint—wrong! That effort severed the nerve in her leg, so she had to have surgery to tie the nerve ends back together. She was able to walk but eventually the peroneal nerve damage left her unable to flex up her foot, "foot drop", so she wore a brace on that leg throughout her life. Except for that, she lived and enjoyed a full life as a young person, graduated from college, served in the military, was a beloved school teacher, married, had a family and lived until December 2012, ten days shy of her 97th birthday.

My sister and I have agreed that our childhood on Hill Road was a perfect way to grow up with lots of friends, and wholesome play that kept us active and healthy. We also had the kind of personal relationships with people of all ages and the kind of interaction that taught us social skills that enabled us to get along with everyone.

Mother Builds Her Dream House

As we grew, the "little house" got even littler! So within a year after moving into that little house, Mother had started planning her "dream house" that was to be a two-story colonial house which was painted white and had a black roof and green shutters. It had an entrance hall, a large living room (large enough for a baby grand piano), a dining room and kitchen on the first floor, and three bedrooms and a bath on the second floor—pretty traditional. It had a large side porch overlooking a spacious level lawn that was perfect for playing croquet. Because we were the only family in the Judson Baptist Church who lived "in the country" it was a favorite gathering place for church picnics! After moving into "the big house" Daddy used the "little house" with its many windows for his art studio. We also used it for storage and play when the weather was bad.

Eleanor and I were very happy to have our own rooms and Mother allowed us to select what we wanted in our room. Eleanor had an antique bed and other family pieces in her room. But, much to my pleasure, Mother took me shopping for some furniture! I selected a bed, desk, and a chest of drawers that were painted tan and apple green with flowers painted on the headboard and drawers. Looking back, I am surprised that Mother let me have that selection, but I LIKED it! As a matter of fact, I still have the little desk (but the paint has been taken off!)

We also enjoyed having our cousins come for a visit on Sunday afternoons. My Uncle Elbert had three daughters: Marjorie, Dorothy, and Martha Ann. Another girl, Janie was born when I was a teenager. Their mother was Aunt Clara. Then there was Uncle Harry and Aunt Elizabeth who had two children: Harry, Jr. (nicknamed "Pickie") and a daughter Jean. Aunt Ethel and her family visited us only one time that I can remember. I guess that was because they had only one daughter, Marie, and three boys: Louis, Jr., George A., and Harry Earl. Marie was a few months older than I and she cried a lot—I don't know why.

To get groceries we had to go about six miles into Nashville on Franklin Pike (that became Eighth Avenue) going into downtown. There was an H.G. Hill Store at Douglas Corner across from Judson Church, a drugstore next to Hill's and Little's filling station a mile or so south on Franklin Pike. Sometimes if mother needed something she would have Daddy stop on his way home from work. If we had to wait for Daddy to pick us up at Douglas Corner we usually sat on a stone wall in front of a big house on Eighth Avenue.

At least one Saturday a month Mother and Eleanor and I would drive downtown to meet Daddy and go to Mocker's for lunch, then to a movie or vaudeville show. Mother would often go to a meat market to purchase fish or a beef roast before we went back home. When she started taking sewing lessons at Watkins she would also take advantage of being near a department store to purchase fabric and sewing needs, or take us shopping for clothes. When we had a garden she learned to make jelly and preserves and sometimes canned beans and peas. Both of my parents really enjoyed living "in the country" in spite of some of the inconveniences.

In "downtown" Brentwood (two miles south) there was a post office, a little grocery store, a fruit stand owned by Mr. Formosa, a little bald-headed Italian man. There was a blacksmith shop on Granny White Pike west of Brentwood a mile or so from Franklin Pike. That is where I rode to get my pony shod—about four miles from home. But, that was in the days when children could go almost anywhere without being afraid or their families being worried that "something might happen to them."

Where Did We Go to Church?

In Brentwood there was a Methodist Church, and a Church of Christ farther on out Franklin Road. But since Mother and Daddy were members of a Baptist Church they chose to join Judson Baptist Church near downtown Nashville. We went every Sunday, but on Sunday nights, if we couldn't get to Judson, Eleanor and I went to the Methodist Church with some of our friends. They had the Epworth League—a program for kids and teens. We didn't go very often but the Morgan family invited us to go with their kids and we always enjoyed it. The Jackson family attended there also but it was not a regular thing. Daddy became a deacon at Judson, and both Mother and Daddy taught Bible classes. I can remember them studying their lessons every Saturday, reading and making notes (a good example for us.)

(I am including this story at the request of my daughter, Jan:)

In the "olden days" the Brentwood Methodist Church was located in Brentwood on the south side of Church Street and just a short distance from Franklin Road. They had a large lawn where they had festivals and picnics in the summer time. One time they included a horse and pony show as part of the entertainment. So, I decided to ride Buddy, my five-gaited pony, and fortunately I won a prize for "the Best of Show." The prize was a leather pony whip. I was thrilled. But then a couple of weeks later I went with my mother downtown Nashville to shop. We went into a Woolworth store on Fifth Avenue, and Mother had something she wanted to get at the back of the store and I wandered around looking at various things. Then I noticed the candy display and knew that the nickel that I had would buy a package of peanuts. I bought one even though my mother had told me not to buy anything to eat! But I ate the peanuts very quickly, thinking that she would not notice! But when she came up to get me to start home, she apparently smelled peanuts on my breath, or saw the salt on my lips! She confronted me with a good scolding. But it didn't stop there! When we got home she came to my room with that pony whip and gave me a lashing on my legs! Wow—it really hurt! Not only my legs but my pride! Needless to say that I didn't do anything behind her back ever again!

Some of the members of Judson Baptist Church that I remember were Mr. Charlie Edmondson and his sister Miss Maggie, Mr. John Gupton and his son Will Ed and their families, Willie and Andrew Tanner, Mrs. Glenn, John Carter who was the choir director, the Hessey family, Mrs. Ramsey and daughters Gladys and an older sister, and a brother Charles, who was a very outstanding church leader. There were also the Dennings, the Osborns, and Vivian Gibson who played the violin with Daddy once in a while. I remember a Sunday school teacher who was nice but very boring as she just sat and read to us word for word from a book. We sometimes had sword drills (looking up Scriptures), and "the battle of the sexes" pitting the boys against the girls seeing who could find a scripture first.

I made my profession of faith when I was twelve. I remember hearing the preacher, Rev. Grimsley, talking about the terrible crucifixion of Jesus and it broke my heart. I thought that if Jesus could die for me that I could live for him and so I went to the front of the church and told the preacher that I wanted to make my profession of faith in Jesus Christ. I was all by myself but I didn't seem to feel alone. I have never regretted that decision even though I was dreading the fact that I would be baptized (by immersion) the following Sunday evening! In those days most churches of all denominations had worship services on Sunday evening.

We had Training Union on Sunday evening before worship services. We were divided by age groups. I was in the teen group and was usually in charge of making daily Bible reading reminders for everyone. I often spent all Sunday afternoons cutting and pasting colorful cards with the list of Scriptures for the coming week. I suppose that is where I honed my skills in standing on my feet and talking to a group. I was selected to be the speaker for the youth at a meeting one Sunday night at a Methodist church in the area.

I remember standing at the pulpit and looking out into a sea of faces, but I have no idea what I said. And, it is just as well.

My Sunday school class met in a basement room and we could look out the window and see the pastor's manse down the street. One morning I looked out and saw him on the front porch reading the paper. On the way home I exclaimed that *"It isn't fair! The preacher was sitting on the porch in a rocking chair reading the funny paper while we were sitting in a dingy room listening to Mrs. Medford reading a boring story!" My father's response: "Beverly, you are not responsible for what the preacher does! You are only responsible for what you do!"* That was a valuable lesson and one that I have never forgotten!

When I was nineteen I was asked to teach a Sunday school class of about eight nine-year olds. One Saturday, with their parents' approval I took them to a movie. I had them paired up when we went into the movie, and for some reason when we came out, one little girl was missing! I was terrified! So, I made them all stand against the wall of Castner-Knott Department Store and "freeze" until I could go into the store and find a telephone. I called the child's home and her mother answered and told me that going into the theater Catherine had stopped to look at something and got separated. So, she just went out and got on a bus and went home! Her mother didn't seem bothered about it and I was relieved! I will never know why the child's "partner" didn't tell me. KIDS! Ugh.

That was the first AND last of such a venture!

Judson Church holds good memories for me and I am grateful for the training that I received. We had what was called the point-point system: attendance, on time, bring our Bible, study the Sunday school lesson, bring an offering, and stay for church (worship). That was good training for youngsters and we never questioned it.

I Start to School

In the summer of 1924 (age six) I had an ear infection that put me in the hospital. Actually that was my SECOND time to go to the hospital! I had to have my tonsils and adenoids out when I was four (I can still remember the feeling when they put that mask of ether over my face and I tried to knock it off!), but at age six I was more aware of this trip to the hospital. It was at the Baptist Hospital, and the doctor had to drain the infection from my ear. The thing that I most remember of this episode was of my mother by the bed rubbing my feet! That was so very soothing and special! Because of the interruption, I would not be able to start to school until September of 1926 and I was very disappointed! That meant my sister would be FOUR years ahead of me instead of three! It was during that year of waiting that Daddy "filled the gap" by letting me take ukulele lessons. Those lessons occurred because a man named Mr. Grady Moore had Daddy do some art work for him, and then 'bargained" to let him give me ukulele lessons in exchange for his work. I remember going to his music studio, taking my lesson, and waiting on the corner of Eighth Avenue and Church Streets for Daddy to pick me up on his way home from work. I still play the ukulele once in a while.

My first grade teacher was Mrs. Jordan: she was tall and very thin and wore horn-rimmed glasses. I remember her

23

as a very good teacher and somewhat strict. When she found out that I could play the ukulele she invited me to play for the class. So I obliged, practiced playing "Jesus Loves Me" and sat in a chair in front of my class and played. I also played "Yes, Sir, That's My Baby"—the first tune that I had learned because it had only two chords! I later learned to play some other tunes like "You Are My Sunshine," and "I've Been Working on the Railroad."

My mother saved my first grade tablets for many years—that indicated to me that she was very proud of my work! Indeed, my mom was a wonderful encourager. When we got home from school she often had a treat ready (toasted biscuits sprinkled with sugar and cinnamon, and sometimes gingerbread cake.) I can smell that aroma to this day!

We usually rode the Interurban to school. The Interurban was a train car that had a conductor and a ticket taker, Mr. Tucker and Mr. Grimsley. They took their places on the train and saw to it we made it to our destination. On some occasions, when Mother didn't need the car, Daddy would take us to school. From time to time I rode my pony. At the school there was a little stable with three stalls, but the only other person to ride a pony was Joe Thompson. One day I decided to ride "Fear Not" to school. It was a very cold day and the teacher asked me to stay after school and do an errand for her. About thirty minutes later when I went out to go home, I took the pony out of the stable, and put the reins and saddle on him, but when I mounted he reared up and threw me off! The only other person there was the custodian, but he came and helped me catch the pony. But I was afraid to get back on him, so I walked all the way home (about three or so miles). Daddy decided to get rid of "Fear Not" and bought me another pony—a five-gaited pony named "Buddy" that I loved! I rode him to school in good weather, and went to several community fairs to enter their riding contests.

I had wonderful friends! My favorites were Margaret Alexander, Jane Meadows, Betty Williams, Irma Louise Niederhauser, and Rachel Farris. A year or so later Ann Griffin started to Robertson Academy and she remained my good friend for the rest of her life. At some point Jane and Betty and Rachel were taken out of Robertson to attend a private school called Peabody.

I liked all of my teachers: Mrs. Jordan, Miss Ella Fontaine, Mrs. Pollard, Mary Sneed Jones, Miss Mary Watson, and Mrs. Bohannon who was the eighth grade teacher and also the school principal.

Of course, "recess" was my favorite time of the day! We played "crack-the-whip," "red rover-red rover," dodge ball and other group games. When I was twelve the school put up a basketball goal and we played basketball. I always got to be a forward because I was pretty good at getting the ball in the hoop. I liked the game so much I hoped that I could be able to play in high school and college—and I did, but we didn't have inter-school competitions.

We didn't have a cafeteria at Robertson Academy so we had to take our lunch to school. Mother always prepared a good lunch for us. She was a member of the Home Demonstration Club of Brentwood and they had programs on good nutrition. When I was in the eighth grade, my mother and a few other mothers decided to prepare a hot lunch for the eighth graders. It was a good idea but it didn't last long as there were too many complications in preparing and serving a hot meal to a bunch of kids!

Eighth Grade Graduation

Our final eighth grade exams took place in April with great expectations for our graduation. I had always been a good student, and "Pinky" Lipscomb and I were rivals. When Mrs. Bohannon came before the class to announce who would be the valedictorian of the class (the highest honor) we were holding our breaths! She said "I have the final grades and need to announce that the highest grades were made by someone whose name begins with a "P" (Pickup and Pinky). Then she said, "Beverly you will serve and give your speech as the Salutatorian, and Pinky will serve as the Valedictorian!" I don't remember being disappointed. All of us were excited about graduating and starting to high school. But then…. a tragedy occurred! The school burned down one night in early May. All that was left were the stone steps that led up to the school!

I have forgotten what arrangements were made for how we would finish out the school year, but I do remember that when our class was discussing our graduation exercises that we unanimously voted to have our graduation on the old steps! Some of the fathers brought greenery and placed it all around the steps and set up some lights for an evening event. The girls all had "fancy" dresses and the boys wore suits. Since I was the Salutatorian I had the first speech. I can remember as though it was yesterday standing before the parents and siblings seated in chairs facing us, and candle flies flying all around. Pinky's father had a long prayer of invocation (at least it seemed long to me because I was anxious to get my memorized speech over with!), I stood up, looked out into the night sky and began my speech with the words from **Ecclesiastes 3:1**, "To everything there is a season, and a time to every purpose under the heaven: a time to be born, and a time to die, a time to plant and a time to….." Of course I thought it was referring to the time to "graduate and start to high school." The speech was chosen by the principal, Mrs. Bohannon for me to memorize. I think that I did pretty well—at least I didn't forget the words!

Of that class I remember that Pinky Lipscomb became a prominent physician; Joe Thompson became a successful insurance executive and a WWII Army Pilot (Tiger Joe); Robert Stamps married my first playmate, Sue Perkins Craig, and was a successful insurance business man; Margaret Alexander became a school teacher; Ann Griffin became a secretary at National Life Insurance Company; John Lellyett Farris became a banker; Frank Morgan became a successful insurance executive in Florida.

The Great Depression

I will never know why it was called "the Great Depression" as there was nothing great about it for most families. It didn't really hit us until the summer of 1931. I had graduated from the eighth grade and was making big plans for going to high school. Eleanor had just graduated from Central High and hopeful of going to college somewhere. But Daddy came to us one night and announced that he was going to have to sell our beautiful house because he could no longer make the monthly payments. A man by the name of Mr. Jerry Mills had offered to buy our house for what Dad owed on the mortgage and Daddy was trying to find a solution to where we would live. Fortunately, believing the importance of owning property (present day Copperfield subdivision), some years earlier he had purchased twenty six acres of land a few miles down the road—a place that we called "the farm"—a lovely piece of land with a creek where we went for a picnic, wading, or gathering persimmons in the fall. Mr. Mills gave us only two weeks to move before he would take possession of our house. Daddy found a man who built us a twenty foot square frame house on "the farm," covered it with tarpaper for insulation, and thought maybe we could live there until they could get enough money to build a new house. The cash that he got from Mr. Mills after he paid off the mortgage was enough to cover the cost of the new place and storage for our furniture. So, we moved again! It was a very sad day for all of us.

The tar-paper house was a very humble abode, but I don't remember being unhappy except that I had to give up my pony. But since I would be starting to high school and not riding to school any more it was okay with me to let Buddy go.

Eleanor was the high school valedictorian and able to get a scholarship to attend David Lipscomb College—at that time a two-year college (it is now a university). I don't remember any complications with transportation—we had one car, the bus from Franklin to Nashville that made a stop in Brentwood about two miles from home. Eleanor had learned to drive, so we had to work things out from day to day. But we managed somehow and I never missed a day at school—and neither did she!

It was during that time that Daddy began spending more and more time making wood engravings. His commercial business had taken a dive, but he went to the office every day and pursued his commercial career as business came in from time to time. In the evenings after dinner he would go out to his drawing board and ply his skills in making wood block prints. I often stood by his side and watched him carve the designs on a block of wood and then roll some ink over the block, place a piece of paper on it, and begin rubbing the paper with a spoon. Then, he would lift up the paper and there was a beautiful print of a tree, a scene.... It was like magic to me! I had no idea that he would one day become a successful artist who was invited to exhibit his prints in museums through the United States and Europe.

I really wasn't aware of a Depression as Mom and Dad didn't talk about it and life went along as usual. They were masters at making life pleasant—no matter what was going on. We were unaware of the difficulties except we didn't have the spacious home that we loved and "playmates" who lived nearby. We had to get water from the creek for bathing and cooking. Mother boiled it in a large black iron kettle. We had a crude sawbuck table in the kitchen for eating and studying by a coal oil lamp. She cooked on an old iron stove, and we bathed in a tub in the corner of the kitchen, and went to the "bathroom" in a wooden "outhouse" in the woods back of the house. I hated to go outside in the night when it was dark and especially on winter nights.

Mother allowed us to have company as she always had: hayrides with the kids from church, frog-gigging parties where we would go to the creek in our boots, wade up and down with a carbide lantern and gather the frogs in a tote sack and take them to the house and skin them. Mother had a skillet of hot grease waiting for cooking them. She added slaw and French fries and we had a great feast!

Mother also enjoyed having the members of my father's art group (the Studio Club) out for a picnic in the

Fairy Ring—a clearing on the side of the hill where she had a long table and a stove for cooking biscuits and scrambled eggs. In the summer time when the strawberries and corn were coming in we would have boiled corn on the cob slathered with butter, and hot strawberries on her famous biscuits. Those were memorable occasions.

Some years later, I had a call from James Knight, a Cumberland Presbyterian minister in Kentucky. He wanted to know if I would join him in publishing a book of poetry. I agreed and he came to my house one day and we got our "stuff" together and discussed the project. During our discussion he asked me if I had ever written a poem about my childhood.

"No, but I will." Thus the following poem:

The Little House, the Big House

When I was a little girl, we moved to the country:
    Big trees, fresh air, rolling meadows,
    Butterflies, blue birds, and a garden.
We lived in a little house:
    Three rooms, wood floors,
    A coal oil stove,
    And Petunias growing in a window box.
      There were four of us
      And we were happy!

When I was a growing girl,
Mother and Daddy built their dream house:
    A two-story colonial—white with green shutters,
    A big kitchen, tile baths, and running water
We moved into our big house one happy day.
I had my own room,
    A German Shepherd dog, two cats,
    A five-gaited pony and some rabbits
There were four of us,
And life couldn't be better!

When I was thirteen
The Depression came.
    The big house was sold,
    Everything was gone.
Daddy cried, Mother wept,
And I couldn't understand.

And so we moved again -
  This time to the farm:
Twenty-six acres,
A creek with minnows and frogs,
    A strawberry patch and a "fairy ring."

We lived in a "little house" again
Built of wood and covered with tar paper.

There were four us
And we were grateful.

When I was in college they built another house:
        A home of stone and hand-hewn posts
        And beams of cedar-wood,
Six rooms, two baths, a dining room
And life again was good!

For Mom and Dad made life a joy
No matter what we had
Or where we lived or whom we knew
Or if the times were bad.
  We read good books by candle light
And the Bible every morn.
  We picnicked in the fairy ring
And planted beans and corn.
  We seined for minnows in the stream
And gigged for frogs at night,
And in the Spring the dogwoods bloomed -
  It was a lovely sight!

It wasn't until I moved away and made it on my own
That I knew my parents had a gift
For making life adventuresome!
They trusted in their God as they lived from day to day

That Higher Power of Love and Hope
To guide them along the way.
For whether we lived in a little house, or a big one on
the hill...
We had the best of everything that Love and Faith
could give.

(Written in memory of my parents, Ernest A. and Bessie W. Pickup)

High School—Here I Come

I was excited to be starting to high school. At that time there were only two high schools in Nashville: one county school was Central High on Rains Avenue in South Nashville, and one city school, Hume-Fogg that was in downtown Nashville. Mother made me a dress to wear for my first day of school and I was very proud. I loved everything about school: the classes, my teachers, my friends, the gym classes, learning how to sew, the football games, serving as a hall monitor,…My best friends were Margaret Alexander, Elizabeth Orr, Ann Griffin, Cornelia Hay, and Rebecca Moss. Rebecca lived on a street back of Judson Church, and I would often go to her house after school to wait for Mother or Daddy to pick me up. If there was something special going on at school in the evenings, or an activity at the YWCA for the Girl Reserves I would spend the night with her. Mrs. Moss always seemed glad to have me there as I was a good listener to all of her stories! Sometimes Jane Gooch, another friend, would join us and there would be three of us in one bed. They just had three bedrooms so it was somewhat crowded, but Mrs. Moss didn't seem to mind—in fact she seemed to enjoy having us there.

Cornelia and Ann and I often did things together: stay for a football game, attend a Girl Reserve meeting at the YWCA, or go to Nashville to shop or see a movie. Cornelia's mom liked for me to come home with Cornelia and she most always prepared a pineapple upside down cake because she knew that was my favorite! In September we went to the State Fair together. The Fairgrounds were across the street from the school and one time a policeman let us climb over the fence so we didn't have to pay! I sometimes spent the night with Ann, whose mother was a very talented soprano and sang with a group at Belmont Methodist Church. Cornelia's father was the famous Judge Hay who was an announcer for WSM and introduced the name "The Grand Ole Opry" on a Saturday afternoon and it has been called that ever since. He was finally recognized for that and now his name is on the Hall of Fame at the Opry House. Judge Hay's sister Aunt Vera took Cornelia and me to South Carolina one time but I don't remember many of the details, except that she was a jovial lady and we had a good time. Cornelia was the first of my friends to get married—and moved to California.

Rebecca, Jane and I became life-long friends. Elizabeth Orr was an "after high school" friend until the family moved to Columbia, Tennessee, and even then, we saw each other from time to time with "spend the night" parties at her home in Columbia. She was the second of our "group" to get married and move away so we eventually lost touch. Irma Louise Neiderhauser and I stayed good friends too, but we didn't "double-date" as the rest of us did. Of those friends,

Jane and Rebecca were bridesmaids in my wedding, and Ann was a "pourer" at the reception. Jane, Rebecca, Ann, and I took several trips together even after we got married: one time we went to Florida to visit Ann and her husband at their Florida home, and one time we all went to North Carolina to visit Rebecca and her husband, and other time we took a trip to Washington to see Jane's sister Margaret. When Rebecca became ill with cancer, Jane and I drove over to see her not too long before her death, and I attended her funeral a few months later. Jane developed cancer a few years later and died in 1995. I am the only one who is still living (2014).

When I was a junior we had an election for school officers. I was asked to run for vice-president and I ran against a good friend, Margaret Alexander and that was hard to do. They always had a boy for president. I remember going into the principal's office and asking him why I couldn't run for president (I didn't want to compete with my friend Margaret). Mr. Brandon said "No—we don't elect a girl for president—that's just the way it is." I won the election and I cried because of my friendship with Margaret, but she was a good sport and it didn't seem to bother her and we remained friends. Robert Macon was elected student body president.

That proved to be a good experience as vice-president because one of my duties was to preside over the student government sessions where we had to pass judgment on those who were charged with some offense (frequently being late, skipping school, starting a fight, sassing a teacher, etc.) The school president presided over the student body meetings, and if he wasn't there the job was mine. So, I learned a lot about presiding over various meetings. I also served as president of the Girl Reserve Club that met downtown once a month.

One thing that happened that hurt me occurred in a math class. The teacher, Mr. Hooper always stood at the door until time for the class to begin and once in your seat you were not to move. If anyone was late he would not let them in. One time as he was coming to the front to begin the class, Elizabeth Orr had asked me if I had a handkerchief, so I handed her one. Mr. Hooper saw me and said "Miss Pickup, just because you are a student body officer doesn't give you any special privileges!" I think that I cried for the rest of the class. I never apologized to him because I didn't think that I had done anything wrong!

When I graduated there were four girls who had the highest grades: Lorene Albright and Mabel Hamblen tied for valedictorian, and Margaret and I tied for salutatorian. Again—I came in second. And where was Pinky Lipscomb? His family sent him to a private school and on to Vanderbilt.

I had the honor of receiving the DAR (good citizenship) medal at our graduation that took place at the

War Memorial Building. (And for our Annual's "Who's Who" page I was elected "The Ideal Girl"—wasn't that nice?) Graduation was a grand occasion but rather sad for me as I knew that there were friends that I would probably never see again. But I knew that I would be soon going into another phase of my life. Where, I wasn't sure.

My favorite teachers were Mrs. John White (Math), Mrs. Nimmerfall (English), Mrs. Brock (Latin) and Mr. John Koen (biology). I enjoyed playing basketball. We all had blue bloomers for gym suits. I saved mine for many years and it is now in the Central High Museum/archives and hangs on the wall in a wooden shadow box.

After graduation Daddy wrote the following letter:

May, 1937

Dear Beverly:

> *Of course you know I'm proud of you and glory in your achievements, and it won't hurt to say so, but of all the honors that you have won, there is one that has not been mentioned, although it is embodied in all the others—your winning of such a high place in the esteem of other people. I like that the best, and I pray that you may continue to win yet other honors as you*

go on, not for my sake but for your own.

Continue in that queenly grace that has marked your journey so far, and to the praises now accorded you by your parents and forbears you will add of descendants yet to come. You stand in the middle looking both ways—may the future be as bright as the present.

I might say more, but to make it short, here's a check with lots of love from

Mother and Daddy

(He included a check for $500—a lot of money for a teenager at that time! I put it in my savings account 'cause I knew that is what he wanted me to do!)

Our First Trip out of Nashville

I loved school so much I didn't know how I would live without my friends and all of my various activities! But I was looking forward to going to a school where I could pursue my interest in art. By that time America had recovered from the Depression and things were looking up for everybody. After Eleanor graduated from David Lipscomb she went to Carson-Newman in East Tennessee and graduated at the same time I graduated from Central. To celebrate our achievements, Mother and Daddy took the four of us to Daytona Beach, Florida—our first trip out of the state of Tennessee!

I was enchanted with the long two-lane highways going through Georgia. We spent our first night at a Tourist Home (long before there were Holiday Inns), and then went on to St. Augustine where I saw the Atlantic Ocean for the first time—and it was awesome! We got that glimpse from atop a large stone wall on the outskirts of St. Augustine. It was such an overwhelming and awesome sight that I cried! We also went to the Fountain of Youth that Ponce de Leon was searching for, and toured the oldest town on the East Coast.

When we arrived in Daytona Beach, Dad found a lovely house for rent for $15.00 a week. It had five rooms that included two bedrooms. We settled in and then went to the beach where Daddy had been the year before and couldn't wait for us to see! I was anxious to get into the Atlantic

Ocean for the first time! On the way home there was a drugstore where we got a chocolate ice cream soda, then rested for a while before going to dinner. I remember that the most expensive dinner on the menu was $1.69. That seems amazing compared to the prices today! We had a wonderful and memorable week.

Daddy let me work for him during the summer before starting to college. That was a wonderful time: going to work with him on the bus, having lunch together, and learning the basics of art: design, lettering, using an airbrush, various pens and brushes, retouching photographs, etc. He was a wonderful and patient teacher. He always had an apprentice working with him: Herman Burns who became the Director of the Art Department at the Baptist Sunday School Board, Lewis Akin who became the Director of the Art Department at the Methodist Publishing House, Maria Ferriss who was the lead artist in the advertising department of Lebeck's (a ladies store on Church Street), Curtis Snell whose father owned the Tennessee Tufting Company, and Bill Wall, a self-employed cartoonist who shared space with my father for a period of time.

3A 206
WARD-BELMONT COLLEGE
1913-1951

In 1913, Belmont College (est. 1890) and Ward's Seminary (est. 1865) merged to form Ward-Belmont College, a women's junior college, preparatory school, and music conservatory on Adelicia Acklen's Belle Monte estate. It was the first junior college in the South to receive accreditation from the Southern Association of Colleges and Schools. It graduated some of America's most prominent women, including Sarah Cannon, better known as "Minnie Pearl;" Clare Booth Luce, founder of *Vogue Magazine*; and Lila Acheson Wallace, who with her husband founded *Readers Digest*. With this rich heritage, Belmont University continues in the educational lineage of Ward-Belmont College.

TENNESSEE HISTORICAL COMMISSION

Ward-Belmont College for Women

Ward-Belmont[1] was a girls' "finishing school" that was on the site of the former home of Adelicia Acklen. The stately mansion was the centerpiece of the campus southwest of downtown Nashville. The student body was made up of both boarding students and day students that lived in Nashville. I was a day student and rode a bus from Brentwood to downtown Nashville. I then transferred to another bus to Ward-Belmont that had very high standards of dress and behavior. In addition to the "basics of education" we were taught dress, good manners, and other social graces.

Daddy had consulted with his artist friends to determine the best school in the area and chose Ward-Belmont because of the art department. I had worked for him during the previous summer and I was pretty sure that I wanted to pursue a career in art. The art teacher was Miss Mary Wynne Shackelford, and her assistant was Nancy Lunsford. I enjoyed my two years there—not only in the art department but in the various activities. I loved playing basketball, tennis, and hockey. I joined the Triad Club (there were about twelve clubs on campus and we all had to participate.) I was elected vice president of the Triads the first year, and president the second year. I really don't remember

---

[1]Ward-Belmont is now Belmont University

a lot of what we did but meet once a week and plan activities of various kinds. We had some intramural games and activities with the other clubs. I have a little gold-plated bracelet that was given to me as "the Triad Ensemble Girl." I was also the president of the Art Club. I had a major in math as well as in art and was invited to make a speech one day about the relationship between art and math. I have no idea what I said!

I enjoyed doing charcoal portraits and at one time thought that I would be a portrait artist! We designed wall paper patterns, linoleum flooring, did water colors, and learned calligraphy. One of my illuminated manuscripts was purchased by the mother of one of the students. I was thrilled that she liked it! Most of the commercial training that I had was in my father's office during the summer months where I had already learned how to make layouts, retouch photographs, and do hand lettering using various kinds of pens, so I had something of an advantage over the other students. I also went to Watkins Institute in the afternoons and took figure drawing from John Richardson.

Of my teachers I enjoyed Mrs. Norris (psychology), Mrs. Ordway (English), Mrs. Rueff (French) and our Physical Education teacher whom everyone called "Cayce." I don't remember my art history teacher who was from somewhere in Europe, but I couldn't understand her very well and just barely passed the course. I think that she was from Rumania.

My best friends were Martine Bunch, Jean Burke (the president's daughter), Betty Dodson, Margaret Young, Jean Ferrell, and Frances Hargis. Among the boarding students were Lenora Gorman from Florida, and Jean Banigan from Connecticut. I went to Florida to see Lenora one time and she and her husband came to Nashville to visit me. We somehow lost touch after that.

The highlight of each year was the traditional "Maypole Dance" that was always in the spring. We all wore pastel dresses (probably organdy) and "danced" around the tall maypole in the center of the campus. We wove in and out and around until we arrived at the pole at the center, and then "unwove" again. There were other traditions: they were very strict with male visitors who had to sign in and out and be chaperoned at all times. If I invited a boarding student to my home my mother had to sign an agreement that she would be present at all times. We had to wear dresses, hose, and gloves if we were going downtown. One time when I was on my way home, I stayed over a couple of hours in Nashville and ran into Miss Morrison and was reprimanded because I didn't have on proper clothing for "a proper young lady shopping in town."

Our graduation ceremonies were held in May of 1938 in the auditorium with a reception in the beautiful Belmont Mansion. It was another sad time for me knowing that there were many of my friends whom I would never see again. I did stay in touch with Lenora Gorman, Sally Wilhite, Jean Banigan, and Margaret Young. (Martine Bunch was one of my bridesmaids four years later.)

President of the Art Club at Ward-Belmont, age 20.

My Career as an Artist

I really couldn't wait to get started as a full-time employee at my father's art studio! He had paid me (as an apprentice) 15¢ a day (10¢ for a sandwich and 5¢ for a drink) during the two previous summers. Now I was going to be paid $15.00 a week (plus room and board). In the earlier years his office was on the fifth floor of the Presbyterian Building[2] on Fourth Avenue North (the sight of what is now the ATT building known as the Batman building) and sharing space with Mr. Venrick, another artist.

The McDaniel Printing Company was on the same floor and very convenient for Daddy because he did a great deal of work for them and for other printing companies as well. But, when I started full time, he moved to a more spacious office on the fourth floor of the same building.

One of my first jobs was retouching photographs of tufted bedspreads! That meant putting tiny white "highlighting" dots on each little tuft. But, I was happy! He gradually began to give me more difficult tasks in lettering and using the airbrush and hand printing. In those days we used pens and ruling pens, T-squares, and ink to make the

---

[2]The Presbyterian Building was at one time the site of the Cumberland Presbyterian Publishing House and Book Store.

letters. (Now most printing is done electronically.) Daddy was a very patient teacher. He had most always had an apprentice in his office and they all loved him. I have a copy of a letter that Lewis Akin wrote for the newspaper at the time of my father's death.

The Men in My Life

I didn't have any "boyfriends" during high school. In those days not many boys had cars, and I lived out in the country with no telephone. But when we had a dance at school, I usually got an invitation to go with one boy or another and two or three couples would go together. Most of our social activities were in groups instead of one-on-one dates: swim parties, ball games, the fair, and an occasional movie.

When I was in college I dated a young man who attended Judson Church named Hamilton Cox. He was a few years older and had a car and took me places. In fact I invited him to be my escort to one of the Ward-Belmont dances. He was a lot more serious than I was! I remember one night we were sitting on the steps of our house and he proposed, but I told him that I wasn't ready to get married—I wanted a career first. When he married a few years later he named his first child "Beverly." His mother was "crazy about me!" In fact, when I got married in 1942 she sent me a telegram that was delivered to the church while I was getting dressed that said, "Congratulations—I wish you were mine." (I first thought it was from Hamilton, but it was signed by his mom!). I really don't know why she liked me but she knew that I was a "good girl" and I suppose that most mothers have their hearts set on a "good girl" for their sons. I dated a few other guys from time to time but no one very serious—that is until I met L.H. Barnes who was my first "steady" friend. He lived in Old Hickory. We dated pretty regularly, but once in while I would accept invitations from other guys. I had several dates with Lloyd Crimm, the brother of Mary Clark Crimm whose wedding I was in in June before I married in July. Lloyd was very tall and blond and slightly balding. We dated off and on but I think that we both knew that nothing would come from it. I had a few dates with Lee Enoch, a lawyer, and Wade Reeves, a high school friend. I had a few dates with a couple of guys that I met at the YWCA dances as well. I met a soldier who was from Chicago that I liked very much, but that was, of course a dead-end street as he was stationed here for only a few months.

A Mystery

I have to relate a story about a man who worked as an investigator for Lee Enoch, my lawyer friend. His name was Herbert Gupton—not very handsome but a very interesting guy with lots of personality. After several dates he dropped by the office to see me, brought me a box of candy, and chatted with Daddy. Mother and Daddy were getting ready to go to Florida and Herbert told him that he had lived in Miami at one time and suggested some places that they might see if they went to Miami. Mom and Dad left on the following Saturday, heading for Daytona Beach where they had been several times.

On the following Wednesday Lee called me and asked me if I had seen Herbert as he had not shown up for work all week. He also said that he had some concerns about him since the information that he had requested about his "resume" had not come in. My response was "No, but Mother and Daddy are in Florida this week and if they go to Miami and I hear from them I will have them see if they can find out something."

It was interesting to me that for the first time ever, Mom called to check on me and see if I was doing okay and how things were going at the office. She said that they had decided to go to Miami as they had never been there before. So, I asked her if she and Dad would see what they could find out about Herbert Gupton while they were in Miami. The next day I received a telegram: "Gupton wanted by the police here. Letter follows."

The letter came on Saturday relating a story that goes something like this: "Herbert Gupton was engaged to the mayor's daughter and on the day of the wedding he had disappeared while owing for the engagement and wedding rings, and money he had borrowed for the honeymoon, and a new car." I called Lee and told him what they had learned and he said that he wasn't surprised even though Gupton had proven to be a capable investigator, but had not disclosed very much about his life and experience in the field of legal research. END OF STORY!

My Art Career Takes
an Unexpected Turn

About three months after beginning to work for my father, he received a phone call from Mr. Herman Burns at the Baptist Sunday School Board. "Mr. Pickup, would it be possible for me to borrow Beverly to help us for a few months?" Daddy asked me if I would like to work there for a while, and I agreed because he thought that it would give me some good experience. I was excited but a bit worried as I didn't know if I was capable of doing what they might expect of me. I had met Mr. Burns when he was working for my dad as a young apprentice, but I had not seen him since then. Working with him were Mildred Schreiner, W.D. Kendall, both artists, and Virginia Doss, a photographer. I was given a drawing table in the outer office next to Mr. Burns. My first assignment: a letterhead design for the Baptist Sunday School Board! What a challenge. So, I made a sketch and showed it to "the boss" and he approved it—much to my relief. It was also approved by the Board "head honchos" and I felt like I had arrived! I would give anything if I had saved a copy of it. I just remember that it was done in blue and dark brown.

I continued to work there and enjoyed not only the work but the people with whom I worked. Mildred Schreiner remained a life-long friend. W.D. Kendall was one of Bill's

56

groomsman, and after W.D. married, he and his wife remained friends until his untimely death not long after WWII. Virginia Doss was not only a photographer but a writer. She and I were members of a "record club" that met once a month and listened to classical music. The members took turns hosting the event and had the responsibility of choosing the music that he/she wanted us to hear. We would then spend some time discussing what we liked/disliked about the selection. I hosted the group one time and selected "The Magic Flute"—an opera by Mozart and conducted by Sir Thomas Beecham. Of course the highlight of the opera is the aria sung by the Queen of the Night. I get goose bumps every time I hear it!

I Meet Bill St. John

I met Bill on a Sunday afternoon in June of 1941. There were several couples going on a picnic and we met at the home of Rebecca Moss. I went into the house and Becky's mom said, "Beverly, there's someone out here that I want you to meet. He is a relative from Mississippi whose mother is a cousin of mine and she wrote and asked if he could stay with me until he found a place to live." We went into the backyard and Bill was on his knees cranking a freezer of ice cream for us to take on our picnic to Percy Warner Park that afternoon. After we were introduced I proceeded to invite him to go with us on the picnic but he said that he had to find a place to live. He had come to Nashville to work for what was then General Shoe Corporation (now Genesco). We chatted a bit and I told him "good bye and I hope that you enjoy your new job."

The following week Mrs. Moss invited me for dinner—and Bill was there. He had found a small apartment in the home of a Mrs. Keim a few blocks away. He told us that he had started working at a Flagg Brothers Shoe Store on Church Street and was enjoying his work. "This is such a busy town—I am from a town in Mississippi called Brooksville that has about 1,500 residents—so you can see why I am so overwhelmed!"

Since our group was going to Hettie Ray's (a little dinner club on top of a hill out west of Nashville) the following Saturday night, we invited Bill to go with us, and got him a date (I think that it was Elizabeth Orr.) There were about four couples there that night and after dinner the little orchestra began to play and we were dancing. I didn't think that Bill was ever going to ask me to dance, but at the end of the evening he finally did! After a few steps around the dance floor, he said "Girl—you can really dance!" and then whispered "we've got to do this again." (Wasn't that romantic!?)

Bill told us that his father died when he was a sophomore in college and he had to drop out of school to care for his widowed mother and younger brother. They all lived in his Uncle Alvah's home where his mom was "something of a hostess" who planned the meals and directed the servants in the house chores—cleaning and cooking, and the garden. He worked in his Uncle Thomas St. John's General Store on Main Street in Brooksville as a sales person, "selling everything from groceries to ladies' underwear!" Everyone in our group liked him and we were hoping that he would continue to do things with us.

In the meantime he started attending (and joined) the Addison Avenue Cumberland Presbyterian Church with the Moss family. He had been an elder in the little Cumberland Presbyterian Church in Brooksville and had been the best man in three of their ministers' weddings: Arleigh and Josie Matlock, Emery and Ora Mae Newman, and Vance and Annie

Kate Shultz. All three of those ministers went from Brooksville to Colombia, South America as missionaries, so Brooksville was called "the jumping off place" to the foreign field! It was at Addison Avenue Church that Bill met Ewing and Roberta McGee—and that proved to be a blessing because they had a car and took us with them to church functions and to other outings.

Bill was 31 when he moved to Nashville "at his mother's insistence." He felt that he should stay in Brooksville to care for her, but when he was offered the job she told him "that he simply had to go" and get on with his life. Bill was dating a young school teacher named, Mary Elizabeth Heiney, at the time and she begged him not to leave, but he had set his sights on better things! Besides, he said "I knew that I would never marry her so it was time to leave." I discovered a newspaper clipping in one of his letters to me when he was working in New York that told about Mary Elizabeth's wedding. He added this remark: "I am glad that she got married—but not to me!" That allayed any fears that I might have had!

One night Mrs. Moss invited us to dinner at the same time and I was fully aware that she was trying to be the "matchmaker" but I was enjoying the attention, and I thought that Bill St. John was someone special! He was about 5'11", and slender with dark brown hair beginning to recede—not particularly handsome, but he had an engaging smile and a delightful personality—the perfect Southern gentleman! I had been dating L.H. Barnes for a year or more and liked him fairly well as he too was a nice person but I was "open" to new possibilities! That night after dinner Bill suggested that we take a walk around the block "to get some fresh air." I could see the approval in Mrs. Moss's eyes! So, we went around more than one block—and I have to admit that is when we had our first kiss! I was walking on air!

The following Sunday Bill asked me if he could come out to my house to meet my mom and dad. The excitement was growing! Since he didn't have a car, Ewing and Roberta McGee brought him. He came in the early afternoon, and after a chat with my parents we went outside to tour "the farm" and ended up wading in the creek that ran across the front of the property. On the way to the house, Mom came out and met us and took a snapshot of us walking with our shoes in our hands. That was in early July and I already felt that we had a future together—and so did he even though he was about eight years older. Mom and Dad seemed to like him. That was a plus!

About Bill St. John

Bill was the ultimate "Southern Gentleman." During his high school days there was a woman in Brooksville, Mississippi who took the "teenagers" under her wing, invited them to her house once a week. She taught them how to dance, how to treat a lady, table manners, and the basic manners of a gentleman like walking on the outside of a paved walk with the "lady" on the inside "to protect" her, the importance of opening the car door for your date, how to introduce a friend to another, etc. She was very thorough and Bill took her advice very seriously. He treated me like we were on our first date even after we were married. He was a wonderful person and above all, a man of faith in God. After his father died he dropped out of college in his second year to make sure his mother was cared for. After he started working for General Shoe Corporation in Nashville he sent her a check every week and continued to do so until she moved to Nashville to live with us. At that time, another son, James Alvah, also started sending her a little spending money every month.

Our Romance (Continued)

I was still dating L.H. Barnes and beginning to feel a bit guilty accepting his invitations to go out to dinner, or a movie, or dancing, or just be with friends. "H" was about four years older and after a year of dating one night he took me to Old Hickory one Sunday afternoon to meet his mother. We met on the front porch of their home, and she spoke to me but I could tell (sense) that she didn't like me—I don't know why unless she thought that I was taking her precious son away from her! I knew then that there was no future for us! "H"'s brother Ralph was Becky's constant companion. They dated very regularly and eventually married.

In September 1941, the State Fair came to Nashville and a group of us thought it would be fun to go. We pooled our resources and came up with $5.75 and went, had a great time and spent it all! The next day Bill got the news that the company was moving him to New York City to work in a store there. We had mixed emotions but glad for the opportunity to "move up the ladder" and sad because we were just beginning to work on a future for us.

My First Trip to New York

During Bill's months in the Big City we corresponded regularly. He was enjoying his work and doing quite well in sales. In late November I had a letter from him that included an invitation for me to come to New York for a Christmas visit. He would buy my bus fare as a Christmas gift. I got permission from my parents to go, and my sister and a friend Ann Griffin agreed to go with me. We were to be there from December 27 through January 2, 1942. I bought a white dress and black evening cape to wear on New Year's Eve on Times Square—I was really excited!

Bill had a couple of friends who were escorts for Ann and Eleanor for the evenings that we went to dinner or to a movie. But for New Year's Eve the two men had other plans so it was just the four of us. But we had a great time. The crowd was amazing and my velvet cape and white dress didn't fare very well in all of the pushing and shoving amidst the celebration! But we watched the big apple come down at the strike of midnight. That was an unforgettable evening. I will have to say that the crowd was very well behaved—that was really a surprise.

The next day we were packing to return to Nashville. Bill was in the room and during our chatter he took me into the closet and proposed! Of course, I accepted! What a wonderful end to my vacation in the "Big Apple."

When we returned home "H" met me at the station and brought me home. He very courteously asked me if we had a good time, what we did, what New York was like—small talk biding time until he very unexpectedly said: "I have missed you so much and would like to make a suggestion—why don't you and I get married and settle down in the country somewhere and raise horses?" I was stunned to say the least! I took a deep breath, froze for a few minutes and told him that it was a little late as Bill had proposed to me while I was in New York and I had accepted. After a long silence he said "That is what I was afraid of." There was dead silence all the way home. When we got home he took my bags and put them on the porch, gave me a hug and said, "I guess that I took too much for granted—but if you ever need me, I am available." I cried, gave him a hug and went into the house. I only saw him two times after that.

The Engagement Ring

Some days before Easter I got a call from Mrs. Moss saying that there was a package there for me from Bill. So, on the way home from work I stopped and got it, knowing full well what it was! He had written to tell me that he was shopping for the "perfect, blue white diamond." It won't be very large but I want it to be perfect for "the perfect woman." I opened it when I got home in front of Mom and Dad. Bill had been quite the gentleman who had written to my parents "asking for my hand in marriage." So, they were as interested as I was to see my ring. It was a lovely one-half carat diamond in a Tiffany mounting. The time had come to start making our wedding plans.

I Go to My First Opera

In April, not long after I had gotten my engagement ring, Virginia Doss, a friend at the Sunday School Board, suggested that she and I go to Atlanta during the opera season that included two of our favorite operas: "Carmen" and "The Marriage of Figaro." She made all of the arrangements that included getting our pictures in the *Atlanta Constitution* as well as the *Nashville Banner*. I don't remember if we drove, went by train, or flew, but I do remember that we had a wonderful time.

Planning the Wedding

Bill and I corresponded about a date and a time that he could have off for two weeks. Just before we were in New York together Bill had been notified that he had been reassigned to become the manager of the Flagg Bros. Shoe Store in Hartford, Connecticut, so we knew that we would be living in a lovely New England city—but where, we didn't know. His promotion was a real "wedding gift" that made it possible for us to begin a new life with a little more income. He was still sending his mother a check every month and I appreciated that—as it made me aware, once again, of the kind of person that he was!

He wrote to me and told me that he had been able to arrange to have two weeks off the end of July, so we set July 30, 1942 for our wedding. He would arrive on Sunday evening, we would have the rehearsal on Wednesday evening, have the wedding on Thursday evening, and go from the reception to Brooksville, Mississippi to "show me off" to his other family and friends there. We would return to Nashville, and get my things (even though our gifts would have to go in storage), and then leave for a few days honeymoon in New York.

By that time I had selected my bridesmaids: My sister Eleanor was the Maid of Honor; the Maids would be: Jane Gooch, Bertha Stanley (who had married the month before),

Rebecca Moss, Martine Bunch, Mary Virginia Morgan, and my cousin Judith Owen, a junior bridesmaid. Groomsmen were Bill's brother, James Alvah, my uncle, Clifton Owen, Mark Osborne, W.D. Kendall, Bill Beaman, Charles Anderson, and Haggard Ellis. (Bill and Charley were business friends of Bill's). As of 2013 all of them have died, my sister being the oldest and the last of my bridesmaids. Eleanor was just 10 days shy of turning 97 at the time of her death.

I had been a bridesmaid in two weddings that summer: Mary Clark Crimm (whose brother I dated a bit) and Virginia Griffith—a church friend. So there were many parties to attend and I was learning, finally, to drink coffee!

During the weeks before the wedding there were several parties for me:

- Mr. and Mrs. Gooch and Jane had a brunch on Sunday morning at their home, Glenbrook Farm on Blackman Lane;
- Monday afternoon, my sister Eleanor Pickup had a tea at the Hermitage Hotel;
- Jackson and Virginia Lowe had a luncheon at Hettie Ray's;
- Mr. and Mrs. Burns (my boss at the Baptist Sunday School Board) had a luncheon at Cross Keys Restaurant;
- Martine Bunch and Rebecca Moss also had a luncheon at Cross Keys;

- Jean Burke had a luncheon at the home of her parents, Dr. and Mrs. Joseph Burke (Dean of Ward-Belmont College);
- Jean Wallace and Mrs. Ben McGown (Martha Wolf) had a luncheon at Jean's home on Douglas Avenue;
- Mary Virginia and her mother, Mrs. Frank Morgan had a luncheon at the Morgan home on Hill Road in Brentwood;
- Mildred Schreiner and my friends at the Baptist Sunday School Board had a "Kitchen Shower" for me at the home of Eddie Bell Leavell;
- My aunt and uncle, Velma and Clifton Owen had the rehearsal dinner at their home on Old Franklin Pike Circle ("Thimble Thicket") in Brentwood.

Those were delightful and memorable affairs!

Vestiges of the kitchen shower after 60 years: the cookbook that my sister gave to me and laughed! There is the nut grinder from Bertha Stanley, one bowl from the nest of mixing bowls that Virginia Griffith gave me, and the cookie jar from Eddie Bell Leavell (my granddaughter, Jill, is now the owner of the cookie jar, displaying it proudly in her kitchen). And, of course I have many pieces of my china, "Chelsea Rose" by Royal Doulton, my silver (Marlborough), crystal (Rock Sharp) and vases, bowls, linens,…. all from friends and family members.

Beverly age 95

The Wedding

Bill's mother, "Miss Nola" St. John and Bill's brother Jay came from Brooksville, Mississippi for the wedding. At that time Jay was living in Truman, Arkansas and working for the Cotton Council. They stayed at the Moss home. I don't know that there was anyone happier than Mrs. Moss—she always felt responsible for being a matchmaker! And, I guess that she was. She also introduced me to the Cumberland Presbyterian Church (more on that later).

After the wedding reception that Mother had at our house, (in those days churches didn't have fellowship halls or dining rooms) my parents took us to the train station where we boarded a train to Memphis. In Memphis we boarded the "Doodle Bug"—a two car train that went from Memphis to Jackson, Mississippi with a stop in Brooksville. We got there sometime on Friday morning and went to Bill's Uncle Alvah's home where "Miss Nola" lived. They provided us with a lovely room. The folks in Brooksville "ate us up" with love and hospitality! There was a luncheon, a brunch (with delicious yeast waffles), a couple of dinners, and a bridge party (I didn't play bridge at the time but I tried!).

I wish that I had kept a record of those events but I didn't. I just know that we had very special treatment and I got to meet many of Bill's adoring relatives and friends. The "black" folks were especially happy to see that "Mr. William" who had "done gone and got hisself a wife." He got many hugs and handshakes from them. It was good to see where he went to school, the little Brooksville Cumberland Presbyterian Church where he went every Sunday, his uncle's General Store where he had worked, the cheese factory, the Post Office, the hardware store, and other little businesses on the square in the little town of Brooksville, Mississippi.

We were there from Friday until Tuesday when we took the same route back to Nashville and were at home for long enough to repack, and get our gifts into storage. From Nashville we went by train to New York City for the last days of our honeymoon.

The Honeymoon

New York was wonderful! We dined on scallops, shrimp, and fried chicken, window shopped, and danced to Guy Lombardo at the Pennsylvania Hotel, to Vincent Lopez at the Taft Hotel where we stayed, and to Benny Goodman, and of course we went to Radio City Music Hall for a movie and the famous Rockettes. One day we went to Jersey City for Bill to visit the Flagg Bros. Shoe Store for a business appointment. I was not impressed with New Jersey and commented that "I hope that I never have to live in New Jersey." Little did I know that "one day" we would be living in New Jersey!

On Sunday afternoon we took the train to our new home in Hartford, Connecticut. We had a large bedroom in the rental house next door to Min and Janet Carples. They were very gracious to us and had hoped that we would rent one of the apartments (rather expensive!) but Bill felt that since he would be going into the army at any time that we could put up with one room for a while. That meant that we would have to eat our meals out and I wasn't too happy about that, but accepted his decision.

After a couple of weeks with "not much to do" Bill invited me to come to the shoe store to "hang out" and maybe help a little bit. I did sell a couple of pairs of shoes, but just "a little bit" wasn't for me! I decided to see if I could find a temporary job. And I did—in the gift department of a lovely department store. It was the first time that I had ventured into the retail world but I really enjoyed it. The other clerks there were very gracious to me (loved my Southern accent!) and I loved looking at the beautiful items of silver, china, candlesticks, baskets, etc.

We spent our Sunday afternoons touring the region—sometimes on the bus, and sometimes walking around the little adjacent villages. It was a beautiful area and the fall flora and trees were breathtaking. One afternoon a friend of Bill's, Cy Bassett, went with us. We attended a nearby Methodist Church a few times but the minister read (very stoic) his sermons and I didn't like that very much! Besides I don't think that a single person spoke to us!

Bill's Call to Service

Two months later, at the end of October Bill got his "call" from Uncle Sam to report at Ft. Devens in Massachusetts. It so happened that my father's family had first settled in Massachusetts in 1857 and he had a cousin, Ruth Pickup Abelein who lived there. Daddy wrote to her and asked if I could stay with her family until we knew where Bill would be stationed. She graciously obliged. I moved to her home where she lived with her husband, George, and their two teenage daughters. We bonded immediately! Ruth was a wonderful woman and very kind to me. I never was made to feel that I was in the way! She was jovial, and a good cook and housekeeper and I felt very welcome.

Military Service Begins

On November 14, 1942, I received a telegram from Bill saying that he was in a hotel in Miami Beach, Florida and would probably be stationed in the South somewhere. So, it was time for me to move back to Nashville and stay with Mom and Dad until Bill got his orders. I enjoyed being at home but a bit "antsy" about the future, the War, and where Bill would be located.

On December 1, he notified me that he was going to school in Baton Rouge, Louisiana and would make arrangements for me to come there for a Christmas visit. So I moved back to Nashville until I knew more about where Bill would be stationed. On December 24 I went by bus to Baton Rouge and we stayed in a hotel for three days: Thursday, Friday (Christmas) and Saturday. I took my wool coat with a fur collar but it was so warm that I couldn't wear it! Christmas day was gray and gloomy and damp, but we took a walking tour of the city, and stopped at a little restaurant for our "Christmas dinner," that was only fair, but at least we were together for our first Christmas! When we had finished eating, a young couple came over to our table and introduced themselves. With Bill in uniform they knew that we were "strangers in town" so they invited us to come to their home for a visit and dessert. We happily accepted their invitation, not knowing what to expect. Their home was small and modest, but very clean and a "homey" place and we felt very welcome. After spending some time getting acquainted, the little hostess went to the kitchen and brought out cherry pie with ice cream and a pot of coffee. We stayed until about 3:00 p.m. then bade them farewell. Surely that was a gift of God to make possible such a lovely time with some people that we had never met and would probably never see again! On Saturday Bill and I said our "goodbyes" and parted, having no idea what the coming months would bring, and I went back to Nashville.

While Bill was in Baton Rouge he got some training in entomology—the study of insects—here again, not knowing what or where his job would be. All he knew was that he was in the Army and would probably be sent to an air base somewhere. That day came after two months in Baton Rouge: he was being sent to Key Field in Meridian, Mississippi—65 miles from his home town of Brooksville! You can imagine his joy—and his mother's too.

When I came back home from that short visit with Bill, I called Mr. Burns at the Sunday School Board and told him that I was available if he could use me for a few months and he seemed to be delighted for me to return to work there. When I told my friend, Bertha Stanley, she suggested that I come and live with her. She had an apartment close to downtown, convenient to work and I wouldn't have the trek from Brentwood every day! Bill seemed to think that it would be at least three months before he would be stationed somewhere—for a while at least. So I accepted her invitation. She had a nice little apartment with one bedroom and a "pull-down" (Murphy bed) in the living room, and a very nice kitchen and bath. She loved teaching me how to cook.

It was good to return to the drawing board again. But I must admit that I was happy when Bill called in March and told me that he was in Meridian and was looking for a place for us to live. Soon after arriving there he contacted a cousin, Davis St. John, and with his and Florine's help they found a little one-room apartment with kitchen and bath in Mrs. Parker's home not too far from where they lived—a short bus ride to Key Field and only a block from a Baptist Church. I must admit that the "little apartment" was not only little but ugly as well. But it was clean and I was happy for us to be together again. Thus began the second phase of my life as Mrs. William Augustus St. John.

Life in the Army Air Corps

On the Sunday after we moved into our new home (as humble as it was!) we decided to go to the Highland Avenue Baptist Church "around the corner." We were well received and really liked the pastor Ed Byrd who, I soon found out was the brother of a friend, Annie Ward Byrd, whom I knew at the Sunday School Board. His wife was charming and they had two sons about ten and thirteen.

With the help of Florine St. John I was able to get a job working for a CPA in downtown Meridian. I didn't know anything about filling out tax forms but I figured that I could learn! I worked there for about four months when Pastor Ed Byrd called and asked me to come to his office as "I have something that I want to talk to you about." He first complimented me for "a good job" working with the teenage girls' Sunday school class, and then said that he had gotten permission from the diaconate to offer me a job to "assist the pastor in church visitation, and organize and direct a youth choir to sing on Sunday nights." My salary was to be $15.00 a week. Bill's salary was $65.00 a month, so that meant that we could pay our rent ($35.00 a month) and have enough for bus fare and groceries. It also meant that I wouldn't have the expense of bus fare into town each day plus lunch. I didn't have a car, but the visitation assignments were to people in the neighborhood—so that was good. Plus, the walking was good for me!

I really enjoyed my work at the church, and I think that they were pleased with what I was doing. Rev. Byrd was a kind but demanding pastor of himself as well as of his staff, and we all worked well together. The youth choir was a huge success and the people let me know it! I had told Rev. Byrd that I could read music and had sung in the choir at home, but I didn't tell him I had never directed a choir! I purchased a book and learned the basics and practiced at home alone to develop my skills. The pianist was very helpful and before long we had a wonderful youth choir of about 25 voices. I discovered that the pastor's son had a nice voice so I included a solo part for him in one of our anthems and his parents were surprised—and elated of course!

A neighbor, Mrs. Parker, invited me to go with her when she went grocery shopping and I gladly accepted. She was the kind of shopper who went to several stores to try to get the "best deal" so it always took more time than I liked to spend shopping, but I was grateful that she allowed me to go with her.

We were delighted when we learned that Bill had qualified for us to have one of the little three-room houses in GI village, near the air base, and about three miles from the church. It meant that I would have to take two buses to work each morning. But, we would have a lot more room—and it was new and clean, and across the street from the Village Club house where we could have get-togethers with the other residents.

With the help of Florine and our church friends we were able to have a sofa, chair and table for the living room, a table with two chairs for the kitchen, and a bed and a chest of drawers for the bedroom. We thought were in high clover! At least it seemed like it compared with what we had before! We had good neighbors who had a precious two-year old little girl who called me "Birdie."

Our best friends were Jean and Mark Clements from Connecticut. We enjoyed having dinner with them from time to time. In fact, they were the only friends with whom we stayed in touch after the war was over. We even went to see them when Bill and I took our Eastern trip up to Canada many years later.

One of Bill's friends was Joe DeCaro of Chicago. He was small and dark-haired, and a typical Italian who loved his own cooking, but he didn't have a kitchen! So we invited him to our place to prepare "the best spaghetti ever!" It took him most of the morning. He began by frying some pork chops, then took out the chops and put in a couple of pounds of ground beef, added onions, tomatoes, and raisins. That mixture simmered slowly all morning and into the afternoon. He came back about 5 p.m. with a big loaf of crusty Italian bread and cooked some spaghetti. I had made some cabbage slaw, and we had a wonderful feast! He was right: "it was the best!"

We enjoyed some of the parties that the villagers had from time to time, but the one that I remember the most was the Ice Cream Social that we had on a hot summer afternoon. I fixed a freezer of vanilla and made some chocolate syrup, and others brought peach, and strawberry. One couple brought a pound cake, and another an angel food cake. One time we had a potluck meal, and another time we celebrated someone's birthday.

While we were still in Meridian, Mother came down by bus for a visit. I think that she felt that she needed to see where we lived and meet Bill's cousin who had been "our family" there. She stayed only a few days but it was wonderful having her with us. I think that she left knowing that we were pretty well situated.

In the spring of 1945, I discovered that I was pregnant and the baby was due in October. The war was winding down, so in September my doctor at the Base suggested that I return to Nashville. Mom and Dad were elated and said that we could stay with them until we found a place to live. They no longer lived on "the farm" where they were living when we married. That was because with the war came gas rationing and it was getting more and more difficult for Dad to get gas for commuting into his Nashville office. They had found a house on Hampton Avenue in the Hillsboro area where Dad had met some neighbors who carpooled into downtown and they invited him to join their "threesome"—that was a break. So, they sold the 26 acres in Brentwood and moved into Nashville. It was a lovely little white frame one-story house on three acres with lots of charm and "just right" for Mom's antiques.

Baby Susan Arrives and Life Changes (1945)

I arrived in Nashville around September 15 so I could establish a relationship with a doctor and a pediatrician, buy some baby clothes, and a crib—and wait until the big day. That day came on October the 17th. Mom got in touch with Bill and he was able to catch a ride to Nashville in a "two-seater" plane with a pilot who needed some additional hours on his record. He got to the hospital about two hours before Susan Robin St. John was born on October 18. (*I liked the name "Susan" and was very fond of a great aunt with the name), and Bill liked the name Robin. So there is nothing particularly interesting about the name selection!*) It was a happy day for all of us—especially the grandparents! Susan was Mom and Dad's first grandchild and they were ready! Of course Mom and Dad were elated and said that we could stay with them until we found a place to live. Our little threesome occupied the guest bedroom that had an adjoining bathroom, and that was nice. There was just enough room for a bassinet and a little chest for Susan's clothes.

Bill Returns to Genesco

About three weeks after Susan's birth Bill was notified that his discharge papers were in order and he could leave Key Field for good! General Shoe had promised to give him a job, so he started to work a couple of days after arriving in Nashville. We didn't consider looking for an apartment because we knew that the company would be sending him somewhere very soon. That pleased Mom and Dad because they were enjoying having a baby in the house.

In the early part of spring of 1946, Bill was notified that he was being transferred to Washington, D.C. I began shopping for some furniture. I already had a bed and blanket chest, a cherry chest of drawers and a little desk. I bought a wonderful walnut antique dining table and six chairs from Mrs. Young ($5.00 down and whatever I could give her each month until the $275 was paid!), a baby bed and a play pen. Daddy had a wooden settee in his office that he didn't need so I had it refinished. I had made a large braided rug, and Ann Griffin gave me some curtains that were made out of paper that looked like fabric. They were in lovely shades of brown, beige and pumpkin. We were ready to put it all together when we got to Alexandria and I was excited!

We Start a New Life as A Family in Washington

In March, when baby Susan was five months old, we found ourselves on the way to Washington, D.C. where Bill was to be the manager of a Flagg Bros. Store there. It was our first time to fly so I was excited. I am afraid that Mom and Dad were not as excited as they were not very happy that we were leaving Nashville, and especially taking Susan away! In fact when we got on the plane and looked out the window to say "good bye" Daddy was crying—and so was I.

Bill met us at the airport and we took a cab to the hotel where we would stay for one night. The next morning we took a train to Fairfax, Virginia to a beautiful development called "Park Fairfax." Our apartment had a living room with a dining area, a very nice kitchen, bath, and two bedrooms and our furniture had arrived the day before.

We had some nice neighbors: a couple who had no children but enjoyed Susan, a young woman across the way who had an eight-month old little girl, and an Italian family who had two children. Plus—not long after we moved to our new place, my sister Eleanor, who was already working for the government in Washington, moved into an apartment just a block away and that was wonderful!

There was a big problem for me: We were not able to

go to church! We had a baby and no car and there wasn't a church near enough to walk. I spent many Sunday mornings hanging diapers on the wash line and crying while Bill was sleeping (he always worked late on Saturdays). During that year we had no church affiliation and we missed it. Fortunately we were only a couple of blocks from a little village where there was a grocery store and a post office and that was helpful. I just put Susan in the buggy and away we went!

Our first guest for dinner was Mr. Bill Weisiger, Bill's boss. I was thrilled to be able to show off my beautiful little dining room and my culinary skills! I don't remember what I prepared, but I remember what I did (or failed to do!) Soon after we passed the food around the table, Mr. Weisiger asked me for a napkin. Was my face red? But you can be sure that I never forgot the napkins ever again!

In September 1946, Mom called and said that she and Daddy had decided to come to Washington for a visit. It was good that Eleanor lived nearby and they were able to sleep at her place, and we were able to have some meals together. Bill arranged to have a day off and took us on a tour of Washington. Daddy had a car so we were able to see the White House, the Washington Monument, the Lincoln Memorial, and the Washington Cathedral. They enjoyed the "outing" but they mostly enjoyed being with Susan—and she enjoyed them. She was eleven months old at the time and beginning to walk and that was special!

After about three or four days, Daddy said: "Well, we have seen you and Bill and Susan and Eleanor, where you live, and a bit of Washington, D.C., and everything is going well, so I think that it is time to go home!" That was his pattern whenever he visited anyone: enjoy a little while and then leave.

In October Susan had her first birthday and we had a party! Our guests were a neighbor who had a toddler, Eleanor and her roommate, Martha Ann Abelein. Can you believe that? The daughter of the woman who hosted me for a few weeks in the fall of 1942 had a daughter who was employed by the government and worked at the Pentagon where Eleanor worked. They got in touch with each other and made plans to share the apartment because Eleanor's former roommate Mary Elizabeth Herbert, was moving back to Tennessee. Martha Ann was a cousin on my father's side of the family.

That was in October 1946. In December the Abelein family shared a time together for Christmas with us, but other than that I really don't remember any other events worth telling about. That is until February, Bill came home from work and announced that the company was transferring him back to Nashville to work at the headquarters. We were pleased even though he wasn't sure what he would be doing.

We Move Again (1947)

In early March we moved back to Nashville to live with Mom and Dad again. Susan was 17 months old and I was pregnant. We tried to find a place of our own as most cities were still overwhelmed with war returnees, but we found a new apartment complex that was being built and would be ready in a few months. So we signed on. And then waited, and waited… at the end of May we saw an ad by a family that was going to spend the summer months at the University of Tennessee in Knoxville and wanted to rent their home for the summer, beginning the first of June. Surely our apartment would be ready by September! So we moved to N. Eastland Avenue where the house had lots of room. It was old but quite adequate and we had delightful neighbors and were only a block from a grocery store. Susan and I could navigate to the store in the stroller and that would be fun. And it was. She never met a stranger and tried to talk to the clerks at the store and even found a "boyfriend" a few doors down whom Susan looked for every day when we made our way to get groceries.

Baby Jan Arrives

On Friday, July 4, 1947, Bill's brother, Jay, and his wife, Remley, came to spend the weekend. The boys were planning to go to a ball game on Saturday. But at about 9:00 p.m., I realized that our baby was going to be a little earlier than planned! So we drove to Baptist Hospital and checked in for the delivery. Maybe he/she would be a little firecracker! But midnight passed and no baby. Baby Jan was born at 4:00 a.m. July 5, 1947. (*We chose the name Eleanor Jan for my sister Eleanor and Jan for several friends with the name of Jan, Janice, and Jean.*) We were delighted! Susan stayed with "Bob" (Mom's sister) while I was in the hospital. I would be coming home in a few days (probably a week in those days). But when we went home, Bob (my aunt) wanted us to let Susan stay a little longer, giving us more time to get things in order. But in a couple of days Bob called and said that Susan (21 months old) had a fever and wanted to "see Mama." So she brought her home. I was very happy to see her and I suppose that it was mutual because within an hour after she came home the fever was gone! I don't know if she quite understood what it meant to have "a baby sister" but she was very happy to see "baby Jan."

We Choose a Church

In the fall of 1947, we wanted to decide on a church. Bill had been raised in the Cumberland Presbyterian Church and joined the Addison Avenue Church soon after moving to Nashville in 1941. During our years in Meridian he attended the Baptist Church with me, but did not choose to join. But he was faithful in his attendance and the people were wonderful to him (and really thought that he was a member). But when we returned to Nashville we didn't decide on a church until after Jan was born—primarily because we didn't know where we would be living. When Bill and I were discussing which church to join, he said "I don't object to the Baptist church but if I join your church I will have to be baptized again and that "would trivialize my baptism as an infant." I thought that "if his baptism means that much to him I can join his church." So, in October of 1947, I joined Addison Avenue Cumberland Presbyterian Church. Turner Clinard was our new pastor. His wife, Dorothy, joined the same Sunday that I did—they had two little boys and I had two little girls. A week or so later Bill and I chose to have both of the children baptized and we were faithful to the Cumberland Presbyterian Church for the rest of our lives!

Still Waiting for a Place to Live

When August 1 came, we checked to see what progress had been made on the apartment that was to be "ready" by September 1. But it looked like it wasn't going to be! So the time came that we had to start looking for *another* place! Mom and Dad offered to let us come back to their house, but there was not enough room for a family of four!

We had to move when the owners of the house were coming home to begin another year of teaching in the Nashville school system. We found a place with a room and bath, and "kitchen privileges" only a few miles away on the edge of Shelby Park. And we moved again! We were a bit crowded with all of us sharing one room. But it would have to do!

That "stay" was short lived! For soon after we got settled in, the owner, Mrs. Johnson, began criticizing me! First of all she put a lock on the linen closet door to make sure that I wouldn't take any of the linens! Each day she put a day's supply of towels in the bathroom. The next week there were two more things: she accused Susan (not quite two) of breaking a tile in the bathroom. Then one day she discovered that the cider in the pantry was white and she thought that Susan had put Clorox in it! (Cider does that sometimes). Then—the FINAL INSULT: on a Saturday she and her husband were going fishing and she asked me if I would prepare their supper when I did ours, and I graciously agreed. That afternoon I had some company from church so I took the children out on the lawn where Susan could "toddle" around, and spread a quilt on the ground for us to sit on. The company didn't leave until about 4:30, so I rushed in to prepare a meal. When the Johnsons came home their meal was not quite ready and she was very angry! Then I got angry and retreated to the bedroom! When Bill got home at 6:00 p.m. he found me in the room crying. I don't know if we had any supper or not—I just knew that we were leaving!

The following morning we got up and got ready to go to church, took the bus into town, then we transferred to another bus to get to the Addison Avenue Cumberland Presbyterian Church about two blocks off of West End Avenue. When we got to the church, Lorraine Cunningham met us at the door, and the first thing she said was "Bev, why don't you and Bill and the children come and stay with us until your apartment is ready?" My reply "Lorraine, do you mean it?" followed by a burst of tears! So, that afternoon Warren and Bill drove to East Nashville and got our things, paid Mrs. Johnson for our time there and we moved! I was so grateful that since that time my home has always been open to ANYONE who needed a place to stay.

The Cunninghams were wonderful to us. They gave us their bedroom and moved into the guest bedroom (that was much smaller). They had three teenagers living upstairs—but we became a very happy family! Lorraine was a wonderful cook and provided all of our meals; they enjoyed having the two little ones to pamper; took us to church every Sunday—and even had a birthday party for Susan's second birthday! Lorraine also made her a little white pique coat and bonnet.

Our Apartment Becomes a Reality

In November we FINALLY moved into our long-awaited apartment. It had two bedrooms, living-dining room, a little kitchen, and a bath. No one can possibly imagine how glad we were to get settled—at least for a couple of years. We were about three blocks from Hillsboro Village—an area for shopping (McClure's Dress Shop, Woolworth's, a hardware store, post office, and laundromat). I could put Susan and Jan in the buggy and take my laundry down and have it washed—no dryers at that time—and then roll back up the hill and hang the diapers and clothes on a line in back of the apartment, or in bad weather hang them in the apartment. We had wonderful neighbors and they all loved Susan! She was so friendly and always in good humor. The upstairs neighbors would have adopted her if they could have. Whenever she saw them her hand would reach out because they always had a "treat" for her.

On the other hand, baby Jan was something of a challenge to us! She was just a few months old when we moved there. She cried a lot and with mother's help with transportation I was often taking her to Dr. Walker, our wonderful pediatrician. It turned out that she was having earaches! She didn't respond to the antibiotics very well, or the pain medicine. I finally discovered that the pain medicine was stimulating her instead of sedating her! So, it was always a "balancing act." I spent many evenings rocking her to sleep, and when I was in the kitchen she was most always on my hip.

Living at the apartment brings back two interesting comments that Susan made. She was about three years old, and was standing on a stool watching me make her a peanut butter and jelly sandwich. She gave me the following instructions: *"Mama, paint it good and cut off the hems."*

When she was four, we had just sat down to the table for a meal and she asked: *"Mama—can I ask the blessing?"* *"You sure can."* So she folded her little hands, bowed her head and said: *"Dear God, thank you for this food. Come in!"* What a treasured memory!

At that time Bill was working at the Genesco office in downtown Nashville. He enjoyed being able to be at home every night but he was not enjoying working in the advertising department. Bill was a "company" man and believed in doing what they asked him to do. But it didn't take long for them to recognize that he was a misfit and gave him a sales job again—this time in a Jarman Store. We knew that it wouldn't be long before he would probably be moving again to a manager's position.

We Buy Our First Home

Two years after we moved into out apartment we began looking for a house as Bill wanted some permanence for the family before he "hit the road" again. Aware of that, Mother called and told us about a development on Woodmont Boulevard on a bus line. We went and looked at the choices of houses for sale and finally agreed on a two-bedroom house on Springbrook Drive.

When we moved Susan was four, and Jan was two. That was the summer of 1949. The day we moved in we met our new neighbors: Louise and Rob Thomas who had recently moved into their new home. They had a son, Buddy (about seventeen), a daughter Jenny (about thirteen), and a daughter, Judy, age two, the same age as Jan. They bonded immediately and have been friends ever since.

There was only one boy in the area but lots of girls: Nan Walker, Mary Jo and Barbara Gill (a third girl was born later), Bettye and Evelyn Kennedy, Pamela and Stephanie Hoos. They all had a wonderful time riding their tricycles, playing dolls, wading in the creek.....And you can be sure that if you were going somewhere you would have a car full of children!

In early 1949, the members of Addison Avenue Cumberland Presbyterian Church decided that it was time to relocate and move from our old dilapidated church near downtown Nashville. The place that was selected was only a short distance from our home on Caldwell Lane. We were elated because we would be able to walk to church if we needed to, but there was usually someone who came by to give us a ride. It so happened that we were the only family on the street that had an attached garage but no car! The garage provided us with a place to have a washing machine. That was a luxury after having had to walk so far to get our clothes and linens washed when we were living in the apartment!

Not long after we moved in our new home Bill came down with the mumps! He was so ill that his doctor made a home visit (something that many doctors did not often do)! During his illness Lucille Morris, a friend from the apartment, called and said that she would like to come and see our new home. I told her that Bill had the mumps and since she had children that maybe they should come another time. But she said "Well we will come and not go into the house." It was so good to see them as we had been very good friends and we had a very good visit and they didn't go into the house. About two weeks later Lucille called and said "Guess what—I have the mumps!" And….to add to the story: four months after that she called and said that she was pregnant! They had hoped to have another child but she had not been able to conceive, so it seems (according to the doctor) having the mumps had changed things. Yet another surprise: she had twins!

We Purchase Our First Car

When Susan was approaching five years of age, we decided that she might enjoy going to kindergarten at Trinity Presbyterian Church with the other kids on the street. The church was some miles away and not having a car we were not sure how we could work things out. But my father offered to lend us $500 for a down payment on a car! So Bill shopped for our first car that turned out to be a gray Plymouth sedan. But then, I didn't know how to drive! Bill offered to teach me—but NOT FOR LONG! I decided to take driving lessons and found that I loved to drive (and I have been driving ever since!) We had a group of neighbors who decided to form a car pool to take our children to kindergarten. Susan loved school and proved to be a very conscientious student. Two years later Jan was also able to attend and I still have a picture of her in an angel costume including halo for their Christmas program.

Some interesting facts re: 1950—The average cost of a new House was $8,450,. Gas: 19¢ a gallon; Television: $250; a New Car: $1510; Clock radio: $59.95; Loaf of bread: 14¢; Average annual salary: $3800. Bill's salary was around $4000. I remember that a friend of his worked for

Genesco and made $6.000 a year and I thought he was a millionaire! (TV's were expensive because they were a new phenomenon!)

About a year after we moved into our new house, Bill's mother came for a visit. Toward the end of her visit we were at the dinner table and she said, "Do you think that you could make room for me here? I really need to make a change as I am not able to continue caring for Dr. Ward's home and sons". (She had been staying with the widower doctor and his two sons for several years as a "hostess.") We had only two bedrooms: one for Bill and me, and one for the children. So I was in a quandary. But I told her that I thought that we could work it out. But how?—I wasn't sure.

Bill's mother's name was Nola Adele Parks St. John and soon after she moved in with us, we tried to have the two girls call her Mama St. John. One of the girls tried to say it and it came out Mama Jean John. It was later shortened to "Mama Jean."

Within a couple of weeks I had borrowed a single bed from my sister so "Mama Jean" could share the children's room. I painted the room a pale pink, found a brown and pink plaid cotton print for curtains and a bedspread. We were crowded but we just made the best of it! About four months later I came up with an idea: Bill was away a lot, so I would give "Miss Nola" our bedroom, the children could have their space, and Bill and I could move into the living room! So I bought a couple of day beds and put them in the living room (in an L-arrangement in the corner), moved the dining table into the bay window, the sofa and chairs, and the TV into the dining room for our "sitting room." That way everybody had some space. We had a table in the kitchen so that was good for most of our meals and we ate at the round dining table in the living room on Sundays! I still look back with amazement that "Mama Jean" was able to share a room with two children: three and five years old, and manage to keep her cool!

The Blizzard of 1951

The winter of 1951 was a memorable and historical one! Bill was out of town (as usual) in January when it started snowing. But then, it began to melt—and then freeze again. Trees were falling, pipes were freezing, and electric lines were coming down depriving us of lights and heat. There I was with two children and an elderly mother-in-law to care for. Mother and Daddy were living in a big house in the country and had several fireplaces for heat, so they suggested that we all come out to their house and stay till things got better. So we packed our things and headed for the farm! However when we got up the street a few blocks, we got stuck! The only thing to do was to turn around and go back home. It was a relief to finally make it home again. By that time the telephone lines were coming down too and I had no way to let Mom and Dad know! What a dilemma!

The next day Bill was able to get back into Nashville and thumb a ride with the driver of a milk truck who brought him home. Our part of Nashville was without heat and electricity for ten days, but Mom and Dad were without any utilities for four weeks. It almost killed Daddy! He had to trudge through the snow and ice down the hill to the spring to get water, not only for the house but for the cows as well. The pond was frozen over and the cows had no other source of water. The sheer energy that he needed to do what he had to do to survive was overwhelming. I don't think that he ever got over it! He did lose a lot of weight. As soon as the "Big Freeze" was over, he went out and bought a little wood heater—just in case. That little heater stayed in our attic for several years as a reminder of that awful time in the winter of 1951! But we were prepared if another freeze came.

Physical Challenges

We had a few health challenges in the early childhood days! Both of the girls had the mumps and the measles. Susan was out in the street when a boy on a bicycle hit her and broke her collarbone. She also had to have some teeth pulled to prepare her for wearing braces (for nine years)! Susan had gotten so much attention from those events that when Jan fell out of a tree and hurt herself, we took her to the ER for an X-ray—but nothing was broken. Her response: "I knew there wouldn't be anything wrong with me!" She said the same thing when I took her to the dentist for a check-up and he didn't find any cavities. She SO MUCH wanted for something to be wrong so she could get some attention like her big sister! (She didn't know just how lucky she was!) Bill had struggled with the mumps but when he got over it he stayed well, and so did I! The girls' pediatrician was Dr. Ethel Walker—she was the best—so much so that she attended Susan's wedding in 1971!

Two Fine Black Friends

When Jan was born I felt the need for a little help once in a while. I responded to an ad in the paper and a wonderful woman by the name of Fannie Claybrook came into our lives. She was a large, strong young woman with an innate love for children and a gift for cleaning and ironing. I would have loved to have had her every day but couldn't afford it! So, at first I had her two days a week, and then cut back to one day a week. She worked for me off and on until the girls were teenagers. I paid her Social Security which no one had ever done for her. In fact, one of her employers called me one time and complained: "she is just day help—not full time!" But I felt that she needed some benefits just like anyone else who was trying to earn a living. Fannie was a very good woman and I could trust her completely! (More on Fannie later.)

And there was Minnie Eva Luster. She began working for Mother when I was a baby. She too was a keeper! She had a wonderful sense of humor, was very conscientious, and dependable. I can't say that Minnie was a good cook or cleaner, or even an ironer. She was just a good Christian young woman who loved children—what more could we want? She taught us so much—not only funny songs but she had a contagious laugh, always in good spirits, and knew right from wrong—a stickler for doing her very best and teaching us good values. And—all of the neighbor children loved her too! In fact, she became the favorite babysitter of every child as well as their parents! Minnie was very active in her church (A.M.E., African Methodist Episcopal). The church honored her by electing her to attend a big meeting in Philadelphia. So my mother invited all of the children that Minnie had "baby-sat" to a party in her honor, and we presented her with a Money Tree—a branch filled with dollar bills that the parents had sent. I think that we were able to give her over $50! (that was a lot of money in the 1950's—more than she could earn in a week).

A Family Member Comes for a Visit

One day I had a call from Bill's brother, Ernest St. John, who was in the Merchant Marines. He and his wife, Alberta, and son, Jimmy, were coming to Nashville for a short visit. They had been living in a New York apartment and it was amazing to see little Jimmy, age 6, at play. He had never had a yard to play in, or a creek to wade in and he was ecstatic! He didn't want to leave. I had never seen a child so happy—I wish they could have stayed longer as it was an interesting interlude and interesting to be made aware of just how much we had to be thankful for. I think that it was the first time that Mrs. St. John had seen her grandson. Her sons were very important: her husband was one of three boys, she had three boys, her husband's brother had seven—and I come along with two girls!

Our Church

We attended Brookhaven Cumberland Presbyterian Church (formerly named Addison Avenue) very regularly and enjoyed every aspect of our new location where there were a lot of young families. The children enjoyed taking their friends to the various activities (Christmas plays, Easter egg hunts, Vacation Bible School...) and the church grew pretty rapidly. I first agreed to have a youth group for Sunday school, and it later evolved into a Sunday night group as well—they were wonderful kids and they all enjoyed each other and worked together very well.

One Easter Sunday we were on our way home from church and the girls were standing up in the back (long before seat belts!). Jan (age five) asked a question: "Mama, what does 'Alleluia' mean?" Before I could come up with an answer Susan (age seven) retorted: "Silly! Everybody knows what that means! That's the way in the olden days people said 'Ha-ha-ha!'" Come to think about it—she was right!

A Wonderful Gift

Our years on Springbrook Drive were very happy years. The children started to school—Susan went to Burton School beginning in the fall of 1951, and Jan started to Glendale School in 1953—both were very good schools. After we had lived on Springbrook Drive for five years, Mom and Dad were concerned for our cramped quarters. Daddy called one day and said that he and Mom had something that they wanted to talk to us about. So I invited them for dinner and after the meal we went into the living room and Dad made a proposal: They would give us three acres on the McMurray Drive side of their farm (off of Edmondson Pike) if we were interested in building a larger home. We didn't hesitate to take them up on it!

So We Move Again

Excitement over having a larger home was growing! But first we had to make sure that we would have water as there were no water mains "in that part of the county!" We found a well-digger who went to work dousing for a "water" spot. He went to work and dug a well that would provide an adequate supply of water for a family of five! I found a floor plan that I thought would fit onto a sloping lot and engaged Emmett Kennon to build the house. It was a split-level house with an entrance hall, living room, dining room and kitchen on the first level. There were three steps leading to three bedrooms and two baths. There was a lower level for a garage and space to add a den "someday." We had a fireplace with a raised hearth in the living room, and a cooking grill in the dining room. That grill provided meals for many "hamburger" suppers through the years (and of course hot dogs, chicken, and pork chops as well).

We shopped for furniture for the girls' room: maple twin beds (crafted by a local artisan who made antique reproductions), an antique maple chest of drawers from Mrs. Young, and a table and a comfortable chair. I let the girls select the paint and curtains. "Mama Jean" would use the little walnut antique bed that the girls had been using, and a lovely chest of drawers that she had brought with her from Mississippi—an old family piece. I don't think that we had ever been happier! And thanks to Mom and Dad for their generosity! What would we do without family support?

The only drawback: the girls would be leaving their closest friends and playmates! But we promised them that they could have "slumber parties" and exchange visits—at least until they had made new friends. That satisfied them—a little bit.

Our New Neighbors

Across the street there was a family with two girls close in age to Susan and Jan: Mamie Eleanor and Jim Keathley and their two daughters: Bonnie and Jennie. Next door was the Rains family with a son, Talton, and a daughter, Harriet Jane, the same age as Jan! Jan was excited to have a next door playmate. We enrolled the girls in Tusculum School. I don't know how they were feeling about changing schools—they never said! I suppose that we had had to make so many adjustments from time to time that they had learned to be very accepting—for that I am grateful.

Tusculum School was only a couple of miles from home, and they seemed very satisfied with their teachers and the school. I never heard them complain about anything—they just settled in and started studying and doing what they were told to do! They were in the second and fourth grades. We were too close to the school for them to ride a bus so I took them to school every day and got involved in the PTA—an activity that I think is very important. I remember that I was invited to do a devotional at one of the meetings soon after I joined. We especially enjoyed being able to walk up and over the hill to visit with Mom and Dad—whom the girls affectionately called Maudie and Bockie.

While we were there we continued to attend Brookhaven Church. It was about an eight-mile drive to church but we managed to get there every Sunday. In fact I continued to be the youth leader. The teenagers loved to come to the house after worship every Sunday night and raid the fridge and play games. We had several hayrides—their favorite party. In fact, whenever we started talking about a Christmas Party—that is what they decided on! I refused to go with them in the cold months and chose, instead to stay at home and cook hamburgers on the grill in the dining room to have ready when they returned. There were usually about twelve to fifteen kids and I loved them all. Then, a couple of years later, I agreed to start a College and Career Class of young adults. They were fun as well and were old enough to take on a couple of social ministries. I remember one Christmas we invited a group of special needs kids through an agency and had a Christmas party with gifts, and games, and hot dogs for the meal.

While we were there Bill decided to join the Bluegrass Country Club that was purchased by Genesco in Hendersonville, Tennessee—about 25 miles from home. He thought that the girls would enjoy swimming in the summer time and he also thought that he might take up golf! They began by making a club house out of a lovely old home and built a swimming pool. Then a few months later the golf course with a new club house was built across the highway. I had a few luncheons for some friends and the girls had a couple of swimming parties. And Bill and I played golf several times and I loved it. But it was a short-lived adventure as the distance that we had to drive wasn't worth it! Besides, Bill didn't "take to golf" like he had hoped. The only time he could go was on Saturdays and the course was usually crowded. No fun.

A Mrs. Tennessee Contest

A year or so after we moved into our house on McMurray Drive I had a call from Mrs. Uffelman, a member of Brookhaven Church. She was also a member of the Woman's Club of Nashville. She wanted me to represent her club in the Mrs. Tennessee Contest! I asked her if I had to wear a bathing suit! After she said "no" we chatted for a little while as I needed more information—especially what was expected of me. I finally agreed for her to submit my name. I subsequently received an application form with all kinds of questions. So, I submitted it and in a couple of weeks someone called me and told me that I was eligible to be one of the contestants. Oh dear… Then I was invited to go to the Nashville Gas Company, the sponsor of what I thought was going to be an "event." But no—I was to go for a personal interview. I dressed in the best that I had and followed instructions re: where I was to be and when. I arrived at the company where the "committee" was interviewing the contestant, one person at a time.

I waited for another week and received a phone call to come down for a picture of the ten finalists. There I met nine other hopefuls—a couple of them rather beautiful—the others like me, just ordinary women in their thirties--I was 36. A photographer was there to take a picture of the group.

The following week a member of the committee came

for an interview at my home. I had to give her a tour of my home; iron a man's shirt; make a flower arrangement; show some of the clothes that I had made for my children; and submit a menu for unexpected guests using "leftovers." I was a nervous wreck! My menu using a leftover beef roast: Beef stew with carrots, onions, and potatoes, coleslaw, cornbread, and ice cream with homemade cookies.

A week or so later we were called and told that one of the contestants, a home economics teacher had been selected "Mrs. Tennessee for 1954." I can't say that I was disappointed—I have a mirror and a bit of common sense. But I will say that it was a challenge and I think that I learned something about myself from the experience.

Becoming Involved in My Denomination

One day I received a call from Dr. Morris Pepper, the executive of the Board of Christian Education in Memphis. I had heard of him but didn't really know him except by reputation. I knew that he was a very beloved leader and he probably knew that I had done a bit of writing for Miss Virginia Malcom, but that is all. So I was honored when he asked me if I would speak at the Sunday School Hour at the upcoming General Assembly in June in Lubbock, Texas. The subject he gave me was "If you teach my child"—one that I liked very much.

Mrs. Mary Ella Kirkpatrick was going to attend the Women's Missionary Convention during the week of General Assembly. She and I decided to share a room at the hotel. During the first night in Lubbock there was a terrible electrical storm and she was so frightened she packed her bags and went home the next day!

The program was held in the sanctuary of one of the churches there in Lubbock. I wore a black hat that I had borrowed from my mother to wear with a black and white crepe dress. Dr. Pepper seemed to be very pleased with my message and that was a relief. In fact, the editor of the *Cumberland Presbyterian* asked for a copy of my talk for publication. I felt much honored. Little did I realize that that would not be the last writing that I would do!

We Move Again-to New Jersey

One night, in the late summer of 1956, Bill came home from work and announced that we were moving to New Jersey! I had been to Jersey City when we were in New York on our honeymoon. I remarked to Bill "I hope that we never have to live in New Jersey (it seemed too grim and dirty to me!) Now, several years later we found ourselves moving to New Jersey! I didn't know what to expect. But, there again, I was committed to Bill and whatever he needed for me to do. So, I was in compliance—but had a bit of praying to do.

Bill had no idea how long we would be in New Jersey so we decided to rent our house—something that I had no inclination to do. It seems that surprises were always around the corner! Bill went ahead of us to find a place to live and called me one night with the news that he had found a house for rent in Montclair—a few miles north of Newark where he would be working at the Johnston Murphy factory. The house was a two-story colonial house on a bus line, and not too far from the station where we would go to get a bus to New York City. It was $200 a month—exactly what we were charging for our house so that was a "wash." We rented our house immediately to a nice couple who were not expecting to be in the Nashville area for a long time.

The day came for us to head north and much to my chagrin Bill had to be in Chicago and I was going to have to drive to New Jersey with two children by myself! When I complained: "But what will I do if I have a flat tire on my way through the mountains of Virginia?" Bill's response: "Come down to the garage and I will show you how to change a tire!" That was an insult but I took it on the chin! But what else could I do? I might add that I have been very independent ever since! And, considering Bill's travel schedule, I suppose that was good.

Bill contacted his brother, Jay, and asked if he and Remley could accommodate "Mama Jean" for a couple of weeks while we were making the move, and they agreed. We had some "farewell" parties hosted by family and friends—it was a sad time for me.

On Friday morning the girls and I "took off" for Washington, D.C. Bill had agreed to meet us there and drive the rest of the way to Montclair. We had a pleasant trip and spent the night in a motel somewhere near the border of Tennessee and Virginia. After we got into Virginia I remember going up a hill and noticed that the mileage meter hit 100,000 miles. Our little old Plymouth was doing quite well! We arrived in Washington at 5:00 p.m. during the height of traffic on a winding five-lane road on our way to the shoe store. I was terrified primarily because it was dark and pouring down rain! I prayed all the way to our destination and was very grateful to be there! I was happier about our safe arrival than I was to see Bill!

The next day we made our way to Montclair and were very pleased to see our new home! It was a two-story brown shingle house with three bedrooms upstairs, and on the lower level an entrance hall, living room, dining room and a little kitchen that had a window that looked out onto Edgemont Road. I enjoyed seeing the cars going by—most of them heading to the station down the road where people parked their cars and commuted by bus into New York City. The house was on the corner of Tremont Street and Edgemont Road. There was a beautiful tall Blue Spruce on the corner of the lot.

We stayed in a motel until our furniture arrived on a Saturday and by Sunday night we were pretty well settled. On Saturday morning, while we were getting our things arranged, there was a knock at the door. A woman was standing on the porch all smiles. "I am Minka Vincent—I live across the street and I am inviting the neighbors to come for a cocktail party next Saturday and we would like for you to join us!" I graciously accepted saying that "we don't drink but we were looking forward to meeting our new neighbor." The "welcome" mat was out and I was so grateful.

Bill had to leave for Chicago early Monday morning so he left it for us to get acclimated on our own! I took the children to Edgemont School to get them enrolled—Jan in the fourth grade and Susan in the sixth. They came home that afternoon full of chatter about everything that they had done and seen, and the kids that they had met. There was one disappointment however: I had told them that they would probably have black children in their school and I was very glad that they would have that opportunity since Southern schools were not integrated at that time. There were no black kids in Edgemont School and they were a bit disappointed.

They also told me that "at Edgemont there is a man from a bank there on Monday mornings and we can take some money and put it in a savings account." I was delighted! The school was teaching children some good habits

That was Monday—but Tuesday proved to be a real challenge for me. I got the children up and off to school even though I was miserable with a high fever. After they left I flopped across the bed and cried for my "mama." The problem: Bill's mom was on her way to New Jersey and I was to meet her at the airport at 10:45. What was I to do? Bill was out of town and I didn't know anyone to call! And I didn't trust myself to be physically capable of surviving such a trip going about eighteen miles through strange territory to the Newark Airport. I finally remembered that Bill had a cousin, Charlie St. John, living in Newark. I found his work number and called and bless his heart—he answered the phone! When I told him the mess that I was in he said, "Don't worry—I will take care of everything." I found out later that he didn't have a car, but he engaged a cab, went to the airport and got "Miss Nola" (his aunt by marriage), and brought her all the way to our house in Montclair! I don't know how much it cost him but he wouldn't accept a penny for his kindness to me that "awful" and memorable day!

I sometimes think about those incidents in our lives when Bill wasn't around to help us and finally came to realize that Bill, although he was an excellent salesman, didn't have the confidence to "make any waves" that might jeopardize his job—always the "obedient" company man, doing everything that was asked of him. I sometimes felt that his family came second! He was indeed very conscientious about his work. But then, I am too—and both of our children are the same way—and that is good.

Our year in Montclair was a very happy one! We enjoyed being close to the school. Between the school and our house was Edgemont Park that had a lovely pond. During the winter months the pond froze over and the girls would come home for lunch (there was no cafeteria in the school) and after lunch they would go skate on the pond before returning to school—that was one of the highlights of living there. Both girls didn't seem to be bothered by having to adapt to another new situation. They were able to "take it all in stride" and life seemed normal again. Our neighbors were very gracious and we got to know several of them during the year.

Our family enjoyed going into New York City about once a month. Our first trip into the Big Apple occurred about a week after we arrived. We did everything: rode the subway, went to China Town, to the automat, and to a movie at Radio City Music Hall and saw the Rockettes. When we got home Bill asked the girls what they enjoyed the most: "Riding the subway, and watching the man throw the pizza dough up in the air, and eating at the automat!"

Another bonus: the grocery store and post office were a couple of blocks down the street, and three miles from our house was "downtown" Montclair that had several nice shops, a drugstore, a very nice store—Haynes Department Store. Bill's office was in Newark, about six miles away and accessible by bus. We didn't go to Newark more than a couple of times during the year. I was meeting Bill one night to do some Christmas shopping. When I got on the main road into Newark at 5:30 in the afternoon my battery went dead! The policeman was very nice—he got someone to help him push the car over to the side of the street, and stayed close by until a AAA repairman came. That was long before cell phones but the policeman asked his co-worker to use the car phone and call Bill at work for me! Now wasn't that nice? In fact, we found the people in the area to be very kind and courteous. The children's friends and their families were very hospitable and included Susan and Jan in various activities. So, they never got lonely.

About church: we visited the First Presbyterian Church the first Sunday that we were there. They had Sunday school for children but not for adults. We thoroughly enjoyed the worship service and the children liked their classes. A few days later the pastor's assistant came for a visit. After some "small talk" getting acquainted he asked me, "Mrs. St. John, are you a liberal or a conservative." I answered "Well, I am a registered Democrat, but I have voted Republican on several occasions." He rolled in the floor with laughter! "No, I don't mean politically—I mean theologically." My answer: "I don't know—I am just a Christian!" That was before I had become aware that there was such a thing as liberal or conservative Christians. I was to learn what that meant some years later!

Since the church didn't have adult Sunday school classes we started attending another Presbyterian church, and continued going there on a regular basis. "Mama Jean" liked her class, but Bill and I were not very impressed with our classes and the people were not particularly friendly, but we continued for the sake of the children who seemed very happy. And that was what was important.

The Beck family (Adam, Dorothy, Marjorie, and Bobby) became our best friends and we visited from time to time. Susan and Marjorie enjoyed each other, but Bobby and Jan didn't seem to have much in common but "put up with each other." Susan had a good friend named Marina who lived in a big house on the mountain. Jan had a "boyfriend" named Carl Schwartzenbeck (or something like that!). He had a big crush on her but I don't think it was mutual! But the kids got together and played in the park after school before it got dark. They also went in a group to an old abandoned house in the neighborhood that they called the "haunted house." On Halloween evening I dressed up in a witch's costume and sat in the living room window with a light on my face. That was because the kids had told us that a woman who had lived there at one time was a "witch." So I made it come true and no one rang the doorbell!

We soon discovered that Montclair was a predominantly Catholic community. The author of the book *Cheaper by the Dozen* had lived there and everyone seemed to have large families. When I went to the first PTA meeting I was almost embarrassed to say that I had only two daughters!

When the first snowfall came the children went to school wearing their boots. I was in the kitchen looking out the window and noticed that a man had gotten stuck in the snow. When he got out of the car the door closed behind him and he was locked out! He stood there wondering what to do, I suppose. So, I went out and asked him if he would like to borrow my car and go home and get another set of keys. After all, I had nothing to lose as his car was much newer than mine! My garage door was right there opening out on the street. So, he graciously accepted and took off in my car. In about 45 minutes he came back, got his car started, and I never saw him again. But a week later—I received a nice "thank you" note from him.

One of the highlights was going into New York City during the week before Christmas to walk on Fifth Avenue, see the shops and the lights, and, of course going to the Christmas show at Radio City Music Hall. Bill tried very hard to make our time in New Jersey a memorable one.

I was pretty busy at home as well. I had agreed to continue writing an essay each month for the Cumberland Presbyterian Board of Christian Education in Memphis. That was an assignment to which I had agreed some years before when I was invited to write for a publication *My Baby and Its Church*, a leaflet for parents of small children. When they asked me, I responded: "Thank you, but I am an artist—NOT a writer." But Miss Virginia Malcom persisted by saying "We know—but we also know that you are have small children and are active in your church! We just want you to write about some of your family experiences." So I finally agreed to try to write three until they could find a "real" writer! That adventure in writing extended into six years and 70 articles! Some years later (1964), they selected 23 of the 70 and published a little book titled *As the Twig Is Bent*. The book also included a drawing that I made for the cover and some little sketches throughout! We never know what we do that might change our lives! I discovered in those few years that

I like to write—and I have been writing ever since!

As time went on I continued to write when I was invited; I think that the first article I had published in the *Cumberland Presbyterian* (the church magazine) was the result of a speech that I was invited to give in Lubbock, Texas for the General Assembly' Sunday School Hour on Sunday Morning—"If You Teach My Child." The editor of the magazine asked for a copy of my speech and it was published. That was the beginning of my speaking and writing for the denomination. More to come……

I also spent some time sewing—making the children a couple of dresses, and their Halloween costumes. But I "drew the line" when Susan needed a graduation dress! She came home one day and announced that they had graduation exercises for the sixth graders who would be going into Junior High School! At that time in Nashville we didn't have "junior high schools" separate from the elementary and high schools. But she was very excited because she had to have a "pretty white dress." So, we went to New York City one Saturday to "find the perfect dress." But that was not accomplished. I remember how sad that she was on the way home to Montclair. But we went to Haynes Store in downtown Montclair and she found exactly what she wanted! And only four blocks from home.

Susan graduated from the sixth grade the first of June 1957. The next week we began our move back to Tennessee.

And—again, Bill couldn't go with us and I was disappointed! So we got the old Plymouth tuned up, bought a couple of tires, planned our itinerary to include a visit to the Stanley family who lived in Cleveland, Ohio and from there south to Nashville.

The trip was "almost" uneventful—except somewhere in Indiana we made a wrong turn and I found myself going north instead of south! That got us a little behind so we found ourselves looking for a motel at around 8:00 p.m. instead of 5:00 p.m.! So, we kept driving and looking for a motel—but it was NOT to be. Ten o'clock found us still wandering. I told the girls that we would just play like we were in a covered wagon going west and accept our fate. Jan began to cry "but I need to go to the bathroom!" About that time I saw a motel sign "No Vacancy" but I stopped in the hope that we could at least find a bathroom! And we did. Then I asked the man on the desk if he knew of a place that might accommodate us. He suggested that the home next door to the motel might be of help. And they were! They offered us a room with a double bed. I NEVER thought that I would enjoy sleeping in a double bed with two "almost" teenagers! A bed never felt so good. We were grateful.

The next day we drove to Cleveland, Ohio, had an overnight visit with Bertha Stanley and her four children: Bill, Gretchen, Carla, and Laura (their father Rip was out of town).We had a delightful time but we did not linger—Nashville was beckoning!

I actually have no remembrance of our arrival in Nashville! I just know that we were soon settled into our old home, and everyone seemed glad to see us. The girls soon started to school—Jan in the fifth grade at Tusculum, and Susan in the seventh grade at Antioch. We especially enjoyed being back at our wonderful church at Brookhaven. Things seemed normal again—and I was still writing for "The Twigs!" I have absolutely no idea how I was able to come up with 70 stories about family life to tell, but I suppose each day is different, and challenges, opportunities come and go, we meet new people, have new experiences. Indeed, life is interesting—and challenging at every turn. But with the girls growing older and 70 articles written, I decided that it was time to resign—for good! I will always be grateful to Miss Malcom who persuaded me to try writing—and I discovered that I really liked it!

A Change for Bill

One Monday morning Bill got a call from the CEO of Genesco, Maxey Jarman. Bill had no idea what he had in mind but he came home that evening with some interesting news: He had been reassigned to another department at General Shoe: Advertising! That was quite a change for a man who enjoyed every aspect of sales. Sure enough! Within a few weeks he realized that he was a "square peg in a round hole!" For the first time in our life together I saw Bill St. John cry! He was miserable—not only with the work but with one of the executives who, for some reason made life very uncomfortable for him. I think that they realized that they had made a mistake. So, back to sales he went! He was elated. In fact, Mr. Jarman, the "head knocker/owner" said on several occasions that "Bill St. John is the best salesman I have ever had the privilege to know." Indeed, he DID have a way with people! His poise and tact, his approach to handling difficult people and problems, and a genuine enthusiasm for his product were the KEYS! I will have to say, however, that they never gave him a real sales job. They give him the task of "trouble shooting"—solving problems with sales personnel, window displays, team work, and dealing with difficult people. If they had just let him "go out and sell shoes on the road" he would have made a fortune. But the company chose to use his other gifts. But he always did what was expected!

132

And was satisfied doing it. He WAS a company man (his "soul belonged to the company store").

I had taken on the youth group at church. We had a charcoal grill in the dining room of our home and the kids liked to come out to our house after the evening youth meeting and worship service (they also had a small choir to lead the singing at the evening service). They liked to roast hot dogs and marshmallows and play games like rhythm and charades. We DID have a great time—and I enjoyed it as much as they did. We had several hayrides—even in cold weather! Of course that enabled the boys and girls to snuggle together! There was Richard Huffman (the ring leader), Kay Drinkall, Darrell Drinkall, Carolyn Cooke, Connie Barnett, Don Packard, Kaye Bates, Susan Weeks,…. to name a few. When the kids went on a hayride I let them go with Bill as the driver, but I wanted to stay out of the cold and chose to stay home and cook hamburgers on the grill! We did have a good time—they were good kids—I loved every one of them (in fact I am having lunch with Connie tomorrow! (April, 2012)

About Bill's Mother-"Miss Nola"

Nola Adele Parks St. John (1875-1959) was the widow of George Augustus St. John (1860-1933) who was born in Allgood's Mill, Mississippi. They had both been married before: he to a woman in Greenwood, Mississippi with whom he had six children: five sons and a daughter. During a Yellow Fever epidemic in the late 1890's he lost his wife and all of his children to that awful scourge that killed several hundred people in the state. He later moved to Brooksville, bought a little farm and "started all over again." That is where he met Miss Nola Adele Hull, a widow who had been married to a Mr. Will Hull, who owned a hardware store. When Hull approached a man requesting that he repay a debt, the man shot him in the back. After his death Nola went to Chicago and took a millinery course (making hats) and started a little business in Brooksville.

Nola and George had three sons: William Augustus, James Alvah, and Ernest Jefferson St. John. George died in January of 1933. Ernest left home after he graduated from high school and joined the Merchant Marines. He married Nell Cockrill, but they divorced a few years later and he married Alberta. After Jay graduated from high school he went to Arkansas to work for the Cotton Council. But Bill, being the older, felt the responsibility for his mother. As I have already stated, she was living with her older brother, but several years after Bill (at her insistence) came to Nashville she decided to answer an ad that she saw in the *Commercial Appeal* for a position with a widowed doctor with two sons "to work as a hostess, meal planner, and home overseer" for the family. She accepted the job and went to Memphis and remained there until we had bought a house in Nashville. She wanted to be with "real family" and she knew that her elder son would be glad to care for her. She moved to Nashville in 1950, and remained with us until the time of her death in 1958—not long after we returned from New Jersey. Her youngest son, Ernest, died in 1957 of a heart attack. He was still in the Merchant Marine. She was sad, but they had not seen each other for many years so she was able to accept his death more easily.

Not long after that, she broke her hip. We had just come home from the store and she went to her room to take a nap. In a few minutes I heard a noise and she called—I could tell that there was something wrong. She had slipped on a little rug by her bed. I called 911 and took her to St. Thomas Hospital for surgery.

She was in the hospital for about ten days. She recovered quite well and was soon "back to normal." She used a walker most of the time "just to be safe" and managed the three stairs to the bedroom area in the upper level very easily. She enjoyed her meals, going to church, and loved it when I left for a little while so she could "mind the children." Life was good again. But not for long!

One afternoon, after I had taken her for a ride, she complained of chest pains. So, we went back to St. Thomas. She was having a heart attack. I didn't know how serious the attack was at the time. About three days later, when I went to see her, she told me that she woke up under the bed that morning! I realized that she was having hallucinations and that was a cause for concern. When I was ready to go home she took my hand and begged me to take her home with me: "You can take better care of me than they can here." I told her that Dr. Grossman would have to make that decision! I kissed her good bye and said "see you tomorrow," and left. That was about 4:30 in the afternoon of August 6, 1959. At 9:30 that evening Dr. Grossman called and told me that "Mrs. St. John has expired." Bill was in Michigan, and I called him, and James Alvah (Jay) who lived in Tampa, Florida. We took her body to the Woodbine Funeral Home in Nashville, and then took her body to Brooksville for the funeral service at the Cumberland Presbyterian Church. Her body was interred in the Brooksville Cemetery next to her husband, George St. John.

"Miss Nola" was a rather petite lady, self-assured, and opinionated—about a lot of things. She was fastidious and always wore "her best" to church, including a hat and gloves. One Sunday we left home and were about a mile down the road and she suddenly realized that she didn't have her gloves! So we had to go back home and "fetch" her gloves—almost as important as her hat! After all—she had been a hat maker at one time. She enjoyed the children, but I think that she secretly thought that I was too lenient with them.

People often wondered why "Mama Jean" didn't spend more time with her other son, Jay and his wife. That is an easy one: she and Remley were not very compatible. In an effort to compensate, Jay sent her a check for $15 or $20 a month for a little spending money. She didn't have Social Security—only a little savings account. She and I managed to get along very well. We were always courteous to each other, and she was so grateful to be living with "William" that I think that she would have put up with anything! She really thought that she was doing us a favor: to be there to help with the children even though I had Fannie Claybrook to come a couple of days a week as needed. Fannie also did most of the laundry (we had a washing machine) and was a wonderful ironer! "Miss Nola" was a bit "nosy" and wanted to be in on everything that we did. If some neighbors would come by for a "porch visit" Miss Nola would pull up a chair to the door to listen in on our chatter. But we didn't have any secrets so it really didn't matter!

Bill's mother was most always in good humor and would eat about anything that I prepared for a meal. In fact, she seemed to like my cooking as I never heard her complain. If I got upset with her about something she never knew it! I would just go for a hike or move some furniture! All in all, she was a very good person and adjusted to her surroundings as best that she could. When we moved to New Jersey she had a bedroom up a long flight of stairs and didn't seem to mind, and enjoyed walking around the neighborhood to get a bit of exercise from time to time. Looking back I have to admire her for "pulling up stakes" from where she had lived for many years, watched as her family dwindled, and made the necessary adjustments along the way. She was very proud of her two older sons and what they had accomplished in their lives as good and conscientious men who "did their jobs" with integrity—a characteristic that she had to the core.

Life on McMurray Comes to an End

After Miss Nola's death in August of 1959, we began to think about a new home. The girls continued to stay in touch with their Springbrook Drive friends and Bill didn't care for the long commute into Nashville when he was at home. I also felt a strong "urge" to get back to the area where the girls would be in school with their old friends, be closer to a bus line, and nearer to our church and school. I think that the girls enjoyed both of their schools fairly well and we all loved being near Mom and Dad, but there was something missing. I am not exactly sure what Bill had in mind, but he definitely wanted a change for us. But I AM sure that the Springbrook Drive kids were elated that they would all be in the same school.

Eventually, in 1960, we found a very nice house on Nanearle Drive off of Franklin Road that had one very large bedroom for the girls, and a medium one for Bill and me. We made a bath with a shower out of a closet for Bill. The girls and I could share the full size bath. We had a den with a fireplace and an attached garage. The best part: the house was on a beautiful lot and there was a Red Scarlet Climbing Rose on a trellis at the front door! I loved the setting! As for the girls, Jan would begin the eighth grade at John Overton and Susan the tenth grade where she would be in the school's first graduating class.

I also enjoyed being closer to Brookhaven Church. I had taken on a College and Career Class made up of a number of college students from Vanderbilt and Peabody, and a couple of working young adults. When we were living on McMurray Drive I had the youth group so this was an interesting change. I especially remember Barry Baker, the son of the Cumberland Presbyterian Seminary President, and John Leonard who was an aspiring lawyer. They both were attending Vanderbilt. There were two young women who were nursing students at Peabody. My tradition of having folks in for a meal didn't change. I had that young adult group for supper one night (about eight). When we had a guest speaker at church I always invited them to come for dinner. For some reason I remember the menu for our first guests: Swedish meatballs in a chafing dish, potato salad, green beans, and rolls. For dessert I had Peach Melba—canned peaches with a scoop of vanilla ice cream. I need to try that menu again!

Our next door neighbors were Bob and Lucille Young and their son and a daughter, Bob Jr. and Janice, both of whom attended John Overton High School. The neighbors across the street were a couple with no children at home, and a family with a little boy. My next door neighbors were an elderly couple and she was rather strange! She called me from time to time to ask me if my oven was on. If it was she would ask if she could bring a potato over to bake as she didn't want to turn her oven on for just one potato! Her husband worked for the railroad and was often away for the evening meal. One day she asked me to come over to see her house. After a few minutes she said "Would you like to buy this house? We need to get a smaller one and I think that you would like this one better—and you wouldn't have to move very far!" She was a "bird."

Bill continued to travel for Genesco. At the time he was working in the Johnston & Murphy Division doing something like a "Trouble shooter," going to the various stores to check on the personnel, critique the show windows, and settle any problems that they had. He ALWAYS enjoyed selling but the company continued to give him other tasks that they thought that he was good at! He was very good at "handling people" and dealing with problems as he was tactful and at the same time very forceful.

About a year and a half later we found ourselves dealing with yet another change! Mom and Dad had decided that they should leave "the farm." It was becoming more and more difficult to manage the cattle and garden. They were aware that we were planning to enlarge our house. They told us that they would like to purchase our house so we could build a house of our personal choice. They thought the house on Nanearle was "just right" for them. So we began deciding what and where we would build "our dream house."

About a mile toward town on Franklin Road a piece of

property was being subdivided into one-acre lots. So, we drove to that area and went up and down Evansdale Drive that dead-ended at the top of the hill. We finally chose a lot at the bottom of the hill because we thought we might have a problem with snow during the winter months. We contacted Mr. Estes and showed him what we wanted—one very much like the one that we had on McMurray Drive, but a bit larger. After his blueprints were approved, the building began. That was in the fall of 1961. We moved into our new home in January of 1962. The girls made a little sign that said "Thank you for building us such a nice home!" They put our little Pekingese dog, Angel's paw print at the bottom of the page!

I allowed each girl to decorate her own room. Susan chose to have one black wall with a long white shelf the length of the wall on which to put her books, record player, and typewriter, with the wall decorated with colorful record albums. The other walls were white and the single beds had red coverlets, and there was a large white shag rug between the beds. There was a large chest of drawers and a couple of chairs. It was a very attractive room.

Jan chose some Danish Modern furniture, floral-patterned wallpaper on one wall and the other three walls were painted white. The bedspread was turquoise, picking up one of the colors in the paper. She too had a white rug on the floor. One day I walked into her room, and there in the center of her new bedspread was a dirty, worn stuffed animal with one eye and a red tongue hanging by a thread. I was aghast! "Jan, you are not going to put that old ragged dog on your brand new bedspread are you?" "But Mom—I love my little old puppy!" "But I will get you a new one that will look better!—he is worthless!" "He's not worthless either because I love him!" Bingo! It hit me that she was right! It was her love for that little stuffed animal that gave it worth—just like God loves all of us—no matter what we look like, how old we are…. Even if we are dirty and have a tongue hanging by a thread! What a lesson for me from a teenage girl!

Up until then we had managed with only one car. But Bill decided that the time had come for him to get a used car to drive to work when he was in town. So he bought an old Ford "clunker" that served him well—and he didn't even care what the Genesco executives thought. In fact, by that time, he too was named to an "executive position"—a reward for his years of loyal service to the company.

School Days

Both of the girls enjoyed school. When Susan and all of her playmates were five years old, we all agreed for them to go to Trinity Presbyterian Church day care. It had a great reputation and was not too far of a drive. She had a happy year there, so when Jan turned five she wanted to go there as well. I have nothing but praise for the care that all of the children had there and they were both well prepared to start to "real" school.

Susan started to school in the first grade at Burton School. She was a very conscientious student and took her assignments very seriously. The teachers there loved her. Two years later Jan started to Burton and a couple of years later they were transferred to Glendale School. That too was a good experience, but Susan had one problem: when she was in the third grade she began to be withdrawn. She did her homework and loved the class room, but she did not enjoy the playground! That seemed strange to me but I found out that she did not excel on the playground like she did in the class room and began to "dread" going out to play. Another problem: the teacher had her first assignment: grade three with 26 wiggly children. It seems that she didn't know how to control them except to "yell" at them and that was very unnerving to Susan. Eventually we were able to overcome that problem, but, being something of a "klutz," she still didn't enjoy "playing games" except on the street or in the yard with the neighborhood kids.

When Jan was four she cried a lot and was called the human "siren." One day a neighbor told me that she didn't think Jan heard very well. So I took her to a specialist and, sure enough: her tonsils and adenoids were swollen and affecting her hearing. So, we had the tonsils and adenoids out she quit crying. The problem was solved! At least for a couple of years, for when she was in the first grade her teacher noticed that she didn't seem to be hearing very well! When the doctor confirmed that her adenoids had grown back I exclaimed: "Are we going to have to have surgery every two years!" "No, the adenoids don't grow after the age of six." That was a relief. From that time on, Jan was a most contented child and happy all of the time.

When we moved to "the country" in 1956, both of the children attended Tusculum School. They adjusted quite well even though they missed their Springbrook Drive friends, but, there were occasional sleep overs so they stayed in touch. When Susan finished the fifth grade she went to Antioch Junior High School while Jan stayed on at Tusculum. Both schools were very satisfactory.

In the summer of that year (1957), we moved to New Jersey, Jan was in the fourth grade and Susan was in the sixth grade of Edgemont School and graduated in May of 1958. We soon found ourselves preparing to move back to Nashville in

June. That too was a very good year which I tell about in another portion of this manuscript.

One winter we had a sudden snow that was at least six inches by the time school closed. Anticipating the snow, Bill had snow chains put on my car, so I was "elected" to go and pick up the kids at Antioch. That was a scary ride for me but we made it just fine and the kids were happy to be at home—I was too.

A Story about Susan

Susan seemed to always enjoy the idea of becoming a dancer or a singer—do something in the "performing arts." She first took dancing and did fairly well, but she decided after a couple of years to abandon dancing. She was not agile and strong enough to take up a sport of some kind other than skating. When she started to Antioch she decided to try out for cheerleading. But didn't make the team! Then one day she came home and said "I am going to do something in the upcoming talent show." "What are you going to do?" I asked. "I thought that I would pantomime "Pink Shoe Laces." So I bought some "polka dot" material and made her a vest, and some shoes with laces that Susan dyed pink. She practiced and practiced until the big event! For some reason I didn't go (she probably didn't want me to) and waited until she came home. She was "down in the mouth" saying "I didn't win anything but an Honorable Mention. I can't do anything!" (accompanied by tears.) So I set her down and told her that "one day you will realize that your talent is in her head. You are a very smart young girl and I am sure that you will be a success in some important field of endeavor!" So, when she started to high school, she joined the debating team and discovered that she was a good debater—making her a good candidate to become a lawyer, and that is exactly what she did.

My Baby Gets Married!

Jan was a senior at John Overton High School. She was a good student and seemed to enjoy school. At the same time she was showing interest in the boys! She told me later in life she admired my life as a wife and mother and that being a wife and mother was her dream. Her first boyfriend was Wendell (the one who gave her the dog for her fifteenth birthday), then she met John whose family lived in the Goodlettsville area (a good distance from Brentwood), and he was my "pick" of the boys that she had dated. But then, through her best friend Judy, she met George who was a friend of Judy's boyfriend. I was concerned because he was four years her senior, but she was active in church, sang in the choir, and was pretty well adjusted so I felt that she had a lot of common sense. But…it wasn't long before she was "in love." So, during her senior year of high school, she and George took a trip to some little town near Chattanooga, Tenn. and got married. We were crushed, and her father was enraged and threatened to have the marriage annulled! But he finally "settled down" and we did what we could to be accepting and supportive. We invited our pastor to come for a traditional Christian ceremony so we could feel that she was married in the eyes of God. She graduated from Overton High School, got a job at a bank and seemed very happy. They found a place to live and life became fairly normal. (Out of that union I got two wonderful grandchildren!)

Susan Goes to College

Susan was eighteen and ready and eager for college. After a bit of "college shopping" she decided to go to Furman University. Furman was a college that was founded by my sister's husband's grandfather, but the main attraction for her (I think) was the beautiful campus in Greenville, South Carolina. Mother had a cousin who lived there and they invited us for a visit when we took Susan there to become a student. And they invited Susan for dinner several times during her four years there.

The first time she came home for Christmas we met her at the bus station. She got off the bus using crutches! We were shocked! But found out that she had broken her foot in gym class. That made for a difficult Christmas vacation as we had to take her to the doctor for a checkup, and then to the dentist and he discovered that she needed an extraction. So her jaw swelled up and people, seeing her swollen jaw and the crutches assumed that she had been in a wreck!

During the time that she was here we were getting ready for a Christmas pageant. The night of the event, Jan and I went early to get everyone in costume, Bill and Susan came later. But about the time people were assembling for the pageant it started snowing. But at seven, when we were to begin, it was snowing so hard that we decided to cancel everything and start home. Jan and I invited Mary Ellen and

Richard Anderson to ride with us, and Bill and Susan followed. When we got to the Anderson's house we couldn't get up the hill, so we came on to our house. But, we waited and waited for Bill and Susan. I was very concerned because of her trying to navigate the snow on crutches! Finally, about an hour after we got home, a car came into the driveway and we could see them coming into the house and the car that brought them drove away! It so happened that Bill's car had drifted into a ditch on Caldwell Lane, but a nice man came along, rescued them and brought them home. We all finally settled in, I fixed us some supper and we had a wonderful evening—and one that the four children never forgot!

Susan really enjoyed Furman University and graduated four years later. While she was there she got involved with an Episcopalian group that she enjoyed very much and was considering joining the Episcopal Church but would like to have her parent's approval. We told her that we had no objection to her becoming an Episcopalian but we felt that she should wait until she knew where she was going to graduate school before making a decision. And she agreed. She added that she had decided to pursue a degree in law and we were very happy about that!

So What Was I Doing in the 50s and 60s?

I was getting more and more involved with the church, and especially on a denominational level. In 1958, after moving back from New Jersey, I was invited to serve on the Board of Foreign Missions. That meant traveling to meetings in Memphis as well as being assigned to some speaking engagements at church meetings over the denomination. The Board met at least twice a year. Within a couple of years the executive, Dr. Arleigh Matlock made a proposal that the two Boards of Missions merge to become one Board with four divisions: Division of World Missions, a Division of Home Ministry, a Division of Missionary Education, and a Division of Women's Work. So, we had many meetings with presbyteries to explain the concept and try to "sell" people on the idea. That meant a lot of travel, but since Bill was most always on the road, it did not pose a problem for me. It was a challenging assignment because most people don't "cotton" to change! But after a couple of years the final proposal was presented to the General Assembly and it was approved. We were elated—primarily because women had had the sole responsibility since 1880 for the foreign missions program:

raising money, organizing auxiliaries, recruiting missionaries, and publishing a mission's magazine. The women had done a remarkable job!

The proposal was designed to draw the total church comprised of men AND women into the responsibility for missions. It meant that the money raised by the churches would go into the denominational budget called "Our United Outreach" to be borne by the church at large. At the same time the women of the church (CPW) would become involved with the total church program that recognized their concern for and an interest in ALL of the denomination's boards and agencies. We saw it as a church UNITED in mission.

As a result of that decision people were named to head up each division of the Board of Missions. So that is when I became an employee of the Board of Missions as the Secretary of the Division of Women's Work. With one daughter married, and one away in Graduate School, and Bill on the road most of the time, it seemed a logical decision for me to accept the offer of a job. It also meant that I would have to move to Memphis or commute from Nashville. The board decided to allow me to commute and part of my salary would be factored in.

Help—what Am I to Do?

I can honestly say that I had no idea where to begin as it was a brand new position. So I just had to make my own job description, taking one day at a time. I first made a list of my hopes for Cumberland Presbyterian Women and become acquainted with the work of all of the denominational agencies, recognizing that we are a part of all that the denomination is involved in—not just missions.

My first goal was for the women "to stand up and be counted" as church leaders: as elders, deacons, ministers… as prejudice against women in those roles has got to stop. Women could no longer "be silent" in the church as St. Paul had stated at one time! He also said, "In Christ there is neither male nor female." The year that I was elected an elder in my church, two families left the church and I was very disappointed. Yet another goal was to encourage women to "get involved" in the Ecumenical movement by working with other denominational women's church groups—and especially Church Women United that included women of all denominations.

I also felt that they should reach out to others through social ministries in the communities: feeding the hungry, clothing the poor, visiting the prisons, and being sensitive to people with various needs both inside and *outside* the local church.

By the time I retired eleven years later, I realized that all of those goals had been reached and I was grateful.

I never had any regrets about making the decision to work for the Board of Missions. The other Division Directors were great to work with! As the Director of Women's Work I was the associate editor of *The Missionary Messenger*. The editor was Roy Blakeburn—what a joy! He is probably one of the best theologians that I have ever known! But he gave me a lot of freedom to do the writing that I had to do: Programs for the women's monthly meetings, a page that I called "Potpourri" that included suggestions for social action, program ideas, Bible studies, "fun" things to do, books to read, etc. I also had a collection of poems, prayers, and quotations on the back page each month. About a year later Roy decided that being an editor was not his calling, so he resigned to go back into the pulpit. His brother-in-law, Dudley Condron took the editor's position. He too was an excellent writer and I am sure that I learned a lot from him as well. He was a man with a wonderful sense of humor who made every session that we had a joy. I will always cherish the years that I had with Dudley.

My job involved a lot of travel to attend meetings of synods and presbyteries, addressing congregations on special days and occasions, and meeting with women's groups in their particular churches. I think that I was invited to about every church in the denomination and I loved them all.

When I had to be in Memphis for one day, I went by plane. If I had to be there for several days I went in my car so I would have transportation around town while I was there. When I first started going to Memphis the air fare was $29.92 round trip (and included breakfast.) At the end of my eleven-year tenure the air fare was $109.20. When I first started going to Memphis I stayed at a Holiday Inn on Union Avenue about two miles from the Center. A few years later they built a new Holiday Inn only two blocks from the Center and I could walk. When I arrived at the new Inn for the first time I went to the desk and gave them my name: Beverly St. John—one lady at the desk looked at me and said "Oh I was hoping to see Jill St. John! She was so disappointed.

The day that Martin Luther King was killed (April 3, 1968) I arrived at the motel around 5:30 p.m.. I was very tired so I went to my room and ordered a bowl of soup rather than go to the dining room. Just before my order arrived I turned on the TV for the 5:30 news and they had just announced that Martin Luther King had been assassinated. I was stunned! About that time the black waiter knocked at the door and I opened it, not knowing what to say. So after he placed my tray on the table, I just hugged him and said "I am SO sorry!" and we had a cry together. It was a memorable day!

The next day I had to fly to Louisiana to attend a meeting of Presbytery near New Orleans. When I got to the church it was about 9:00 a.m. and there were some men standing outside near the steps talking. They knew that I had just come from Memphis and one of them said something like "How are things in Memphis?" I responded "A lot of people are pretty sad." "Well, he had it coming to him!" And, "Everywhere he went he caused trouble." Or, "He was just a troublemaker."

Later in the morning when it came my time to speak I had a hard time staying with my subject as my mind and heart were aflutter with sadness and anger! But I held my tongue and prayed that the time would come when those men would realize the error of their thinking! As most people did after several years had passed. The time came in the early 1960's when Bethel College voted to accept black students, and the Seminary admitted black ministerial students. Indeed, God and time have a way of helping people to see things differently and be more open and accepting and realizing that "in Christ there is neither Greek nor Jew, male nor female..."

I Had a Lot of Help

In connection with my work, I had a Convention executive committee that met at least two times during the year to plan the Cumberland Presbyterian Women (CPW) theme, select related program topics, Bible Studies, and special mission projects. We occasionally met at the sight of the up-coming Convention, or in someone's home. When Jackie Mattonen was the Convention president she invited us to come to Independence, Missouri for our planning meeting. The officers came to Nashville and I drove us to Missouri. About two hours into our trip it started snowing, but we continued on. By the time we arrived at Jackie's house there was at least six inches of snow on the ground and still snowing! Needless to say we were "snowed in" for several days. But she had a very spacious house and we made the best of it—and finished planning the up-coming Convention program with the theme "Bloom Where You Are Planted." It was a memorable meeting, primarily because we had the courage to petition the General Assembly to appoint a committee to prepare a paper on "The Role of Women in the Cumberland Presbyterian Church." We were encouraging women to accept roles of leadership in their churches, and at the same time encouraging churches to consider electing and accepting women as elders and deacons and clergy. One by one, individuals and churches began to change—but it took a long time. In fact, it took the General Assembly over 20 years to recognize Louisa Woosley's ordination. That occurred in 1921 after women of the United States were given the right to vote. Now nearly every church in the denomination has women as elders and deacons, and the number of ordained women has increased immeasurably.

I Receive an Invitation to Go to Colombia, South America

In 1966, I was invited by the Colombian Missionaries to come to Colombia for a couple of weeks, primarily to lead a retreat for the Cumberland Presbyterian Women there to be held at Camp El Coro, high in the Andes Mountains out from Cali. I was elated! The invitation was sent to the Board of Missions, and after they approved the visit I received a letter from Beth Wallace telling me that they wanted me there for at least two weeks. That would include visits to all of the churches in addition to the retreat that was to be on the final weekend.

The Colombian planning committee sent me a schedule of events and an itinerary. They filled every minute of every day to make sure that I saw everything, went everywhere, and met everyone! The schedule called for me to leave on Saturday, February 18 and stay until Monday, March 4—two weeks filled with various activities. I wanted to be very careful in planning my wardrobe. I wanted to be modest in my dress because I wanted to be respectful of a people who are poor, but at the same time I wanted to be an authentic "gringo" (what they call all North Americans!) I was told that the weather would be warm, but I was leaving in cold weather so I did wear a wool suit and took a raincoat (not aware that it seldom rains in Colombia!) Colombia is very warm so I packed warm weather clothes. But something unforeseen happened—My bags didn't arrive when I did! And that posed a problem. Rev. Jose Fajardo made contact with the airlines and arranged for my bags to be delivered to his home whenever they were found. Fortunately I had my brief case with my lecture notes and the posters that I had made for the Retreat. But life goes on, and I just ignored my dilemma and made the best of it.

My first time to speak was on Sunday, the 19th, at the Cali Cumberland Presbyterian Church. Cali Central is the first church that was built in Colombia and is the largest Protestant church in the area. It was full and I must admit that I was terrified, as it was the first time that had spoken to a group with a translator (Jose) but they didn't send me home! After church I had lunch with the Fajardos, and did a bit of sight-seeing in the afternoon. I then went to the home of John and Joyce Lovelace for dinner. From there we went to La Floresta Cumberland Presbyterian Church. It was in a suburban area and it too was full of curious people! They were very receptive and made me feel quite welcome. They, of course, knew that I was wearing borrowed clothes (the person making the introduction told them and you could see the distress and pity on their faces!) I have no idea what I said as I didn't have any "planned" message—I suppose I just told them about my life in the Cumberland Presbyterian Church, when I first heard about Jose Fajardo and something about my Christian journey.

On Monday, after checking with the airport and learned that my bags had not arrived, I went to a store and purchased a change of underwear. By that time the missionary wives had gotten a few items for me to wear: a white pleated skirt from Fanny Fajardo, a blue and white striped blouse from Beth Clyne, and some beige plastic sandals from Beth Wallace. That outfit became my "uniform" for the next two weeks. I found myself in an interesting situation: those poor Colombians felt sorry for me (a "rich" gringo) instead of me feeling sorry for the Colombians, many of whom lived in dire poverty. But they were a very happy people—primarily because they were Christians, and loved their new-found faith, and a loving church family. The evangelical Christians there are called "the people of the book" because they carry their Bibles with them everywhere they go. And their worship services are quite joyful as they use all kinds of musical instruments in the services.

The planning committee had decided that it would be best for me to stay in the same place during my visit so I would not have to pack and unpack like I would if I stayed in the various homes. So it was decided that I would stay at Katherine and Bill Wood's home. They had three children: Kathy twelve, Celia, ten, and John, age eight.

I had the privilege to visit every church in the presbytery—even to Buenaventura, a fishing village on the coast, go to a pineapple farm, go to the Colegio Americano and speak to the students there. But the main reason that I was invited to Colombia was to lead a weekend retreat for the women of the presbytery. The topic that they gave me for the Retreat was "The Relationship of a Woman to Her Husband, Her Church, and Her Community." That was a real challenge—especially since I didn't speak the language! Jose Fajardo was to be my interpreter and I knew that he was very proficient, but still, I felt that I needed some visual aids. After some contemplation, I decided to make a large poster of a woman with cellophane overlays with cutouts of (1) a man, (2) a church, and (3) a community. I bought a large portfolio in which to put them for transporting. Then I began thinking about what I would say. I also did a lot of praying! What a challenge! But, you know what? I didn't lose any sleep over it because I knew that I would have a lot of encouragement and support. There were about 150 ladies and they seemed very happy and quite receptive—I have never had such a delightful and enthusiastic audience!

At the end of the retreat at noon on Sunday, a young Colombian woman came up to me with a little package wrapped in brown tissue. She handed it to me and said "This is from my husband's gift shop." As I was opening it she added "I will never forget you. Please, you pray for me and I pray for you." In the modest little package was a mother pig and two piglets made of molded cotton." Her gift is on a shelf in my dining room as a daily reminder of Noami Villegas and the importance of intercessory prayer. The following day John Lovelace took me to Armenia, a little village with dirt roads. There at the intersection of two muddy roads was a crude wooden kiosk with little packages/boxes hanging on it. John told me that Kiosk was Noami's husband's gift shop! Seeing that little "shop" made me appreciate Noami's gift even more.

John then took me into a little home to meet one of his church members. I don't remember her name but her house had a dirt floor, the furniture was made of wooden crates, and a stove made out of a large tin can .I learned that she popped corn on that little stove, put it in little paper bags, and her children took them to school to sell to pay for their education.

Church Women United & the American Bible Society

Soon after I began working for the Board of Missions, I began to receive invitations to participate in various organizations that provided me many opportunities to travel and meet interesting people.

My first trip was to New York to attend a meeting of the various denominational representatives who served on the Board of Managers. We met at the headquarters that was called "The Bible House." When I went into the main entrance there was a large group of people standing in the lobby and listening to a man who was introducing two ladies who had just come from a remote village in Africa. They had been there for 24 years creating a written language for those people, and had translated the Gospel of John into that language! They were being honored and presented with the first copy of that Scripture! It was an awesome experience!

Another time they had just installed a glass case that held all of Helen Keller's frayed Braille Scriptures that were a testimony to her faith that along with her wonderful teacher Annie Sullivan. What a remarkable woman Helen was—surely she is one of my "she-roses," And Mother Teresa as well. I was later invited to represent the Society as a member of the Volunteer Team with all expenses paid to go to various meetings over the United States to promote the American Bible Society. They equipped me with an interesting tri-fold display and a lot of materials and hand-outs. I wasn't able to fulfill many of their assignments because my other tasks had a priority. But I do remember going to a large meeting in South Carolina where I was treated to a wonderful luncheon where they served the best biscuits I ever ate—and gave me a check for $1,000 for the American Bible Society.

My next "international" invitation came from Church Women United in New York. Since I had the title of "executive" I was invited to attend the National CWU organization and be a part of the Executive Council that was made up of executives/leaders of church women's organizations. That meant an annual meeting plus an occasional retreat during the summer. It was at such an occasion at Montreat in North Carolina that I shared a room with an interesting lady from Haiti. We eventually lost touch with each other.

The Committee on Unification

During the late 1960's and on into the 70's, 80's and 90's some of the General Assembly members had the desire to unite the Cumberland Presbyterian Church and the Second Cumberland Presbyterian Church (later the Cumberland Presbyterian Church in America). But in spite of some of their good intentions, the job was a difficult one, not only for the white church but for the black church as well. There was first the "Unification Committee" and after it failed, the name was changed to "the Cooperative Work Committee." I happened to serve on both as I was totally committed to becoming one church. We even had two very successful "celebrations of unity"—one in Huntsville, Alabama, and one in Jackson, Tennessee .Those occasions made us "feel" like the churches were ready to unite, but that was not to be as every recommendation to unite was denied. I think that I was on the committee for eighteen or twenty years and I became very discouraged so I resigned. The committees continued to function with the same goal in mind—until, finally, in 2012, the recommendation passed. I suppose that the church was ready—at last—to become one body. There is now (2014) a new committee that is working on a "process" to make unity really happen. I can understand the hesitancy of the black church because of the fear of being "taken over" by the white church so we must be very careful to be completely fair and unbiased in the process. Time will tell.......

Another Trip Overseas

I also met Dorothy Wagner who was the Executive of the Presbyterian Church USA women's organization. Soon after returning to Memphis I received a letter from her inviting me to go with her and a group of thirty women from the United States who would be representing one of several denominations. She also suggested that I might like to invite a friend to go with me. So, after getting permission from Dr. Ramsey to be away that long, (we had to pay our own way) I invited Bernice McDonald of Knoxville, Tennessee to go with me and she accepted. She was a delightful traveling companion and we enjoyed every moment of our time together.

We spent two weeks, first in Rome, then on to Verona, and Milan and other places in Italy until we arrived in Austria. This is where we had the conference with the other women and where we heard some outstanding speakers with a translator, of course. We were turned over to a European hostess for the next leg of the trip. Bernice and I had two Waldensian women to take us to meet with some Waldensian women to be together for a time of sharing. They took us to a beautiful library to learn about the Waldensian Church which actually preceded Martin Luther. Of course there are no cars in Venice so we had to walk everywhere—my feet got so tired I went into a shoe store but all of the shoes were very wide so I just managed with what I had! We went to one of the ladies' homes and had some tea and conversation.

Our last stop was in Geneva, Switzerland where we went on a bus tour of that beautiful city, and then to the headquarters of the World Council of Churches where we had a moving worship service. The sanctuary was walled with strips of wood from every country in the world. There were people from many countries there for the service that closed with all of us saying "the Lord's Prayer" each in our own tongue. I was enraptured! Feeling somewhat like the people who were at Pentecost must have felt. That was surely the highlight of the conference for me.

My Most Challenging Assignment

I was invited to be the guest speaker at a national women's gathering of the Presbyterian Church USA. (Shaw Scates, Stated Clerk of our denomination, had given them my name!) The subject assigned to me was "The Reformation Speaks to Us Today." Well! That meant a lot of study but I enjoyed doing the research and I learned a lot in the process. The meeting was at the First Presbyterian Church in Memphis and there were about 1000 women there and they were very gracious and encouraging.

For the next eleven years making speeches, giving devotionals, making program suggestions, sharing ideas for projects for women's groups, etc., became a way of life. I stayed in motels, hotels, peoples' homes—whatever the host people wanted me to do! Any remuneration that was given to me was turned in to the Board of Missions as they paid all of my expenses that included travel, meals, tips, cabs, etc. In all of those years of travel, I had car trouble only three times: once in Alabama when I was only a block from a car repair shop and in Illinois when I was in front of a gas station! Both were very minor problems, and the people were very helpful and charged me very little.

The third time, however, was different: I was with two ladies going through Kentucky on our way to Purdue University and we were so busy talking I didn't think to look at my gas gauge until my car started slowing down and noticed that I was "on empty!" I came to a stop on the shoulder and the two ladies suggested that I stay with the car while they went to a farm house a short way up the road where they would go for help. In about fifteen minutes they came back riding in the cab of a big truck! The driver was a farmer who had a gas tank, so he brought them back with a two-gallon can of gas and put it in my car. I paid him, and away we went to the next exit where I got a fill-up! I have no doubt that my Guardian Angel was with me—not only then but all of the time!

CPW National Conventions

Cumberland Presbyterian Women had a Convention every June at the same time and place that the General Assembly was in session. I worked with the Stated Clerk and the current Moderator and went with then to the Convention site to make arrangements for the various meetings, committee rooms, sound systems, staging, chair arrangements, etc. and all that goes into planning for seven or eight hundred people. I often told people that the hardest part of making such plans depended on the hotel staff and their ability to fulfill all of the promises that they made to meet our various needs. There were ALWAYS problems, but we managed to work them out. I accepted that as just part of my job! I think that CPW programs were always interesting, educational, entertaining, and enjoyable with a lot of variety. We had a theme for each convention with banners, a Bible study, special projects, lots of music, drama, interpretative dance, and, of course a guest speaker to challenge us. One of the highlights was the President's message, primarily on our theme.

The meeting places during the period of time that I was working for the Board of Missions (1965-1976) were: San Francisco, California; Memphis, Tennessee; Paducah, Kentucky; Oklahoma City, Oklahoma; San Antonio, Texas; Knoxville, Tennessee; Jackson, Tennessee; Kansas City,

Missouri; Tampa, Florida; McKenzie, Tennessee; and Tulsa, Oklahoma.

I Retired after Eleven Years

Bill had to retire from Genesco at the age of 65 (that seems so young now!). 1975 was his time to retire so I decided to submit my resignation to the Board of Missions. I told the women that I had had two careers: one as a commercial artist, and then as the Director of Women's Work, so NOW I was going to try Marriage! Bill and I had both been traveling for many years and in different directions, and I was hoping that this would be an opportunity for us to learn to live together! My resignation was accepted, but I agreed to stay on until they could find someone to replace me. Well—that took a year and they still had not hired anyone. But I retired anyway! Dudley Condron agreed to help out until a replacement was found. So he and the Convention president, Joanne Alexander, worked together along with the Convention executive committee to plan the upcoming convention, and provide some program suggestions.

At my last Convention (June 1976) after submitting my resignation, I was honored with a gift from each presbytery, a gift of a beautiful Bible from the American Bible Society, and lots of accolades. It was a memorable but "tearful" time. But, I was ready for a change, and the thought of just "being at home" was wonderful. I must say that I missed my friends at the Denominational Center in Memphis, and I missed the traveling and getting to know new churches and their members.

I suppose that Tennessee Synod thought that now that I had retired from working for the Board of Missions that I would need something else to do! So they asked me if I would be the Stated Clerk for the Synod and I accepted feeling that I was able to do that without much time. WRONG! It was a time consuming job that I really enjoyed at first. But after three years I decided that being the clerk and taking the minutes of the meeting (once a year) was not for me, so I resigned.

Surprise! I Was Nominated for Moderator in 1977

I don't remember whose idea it was but I found myself being nominated for moderator of the General Assembly. I do remember that I invited Carl Ramsey to make the nominating speech. I also remember that there were three other people nominated. One of them was Fred Bryson who was a member of the Bethel College Board of Trustees and had made a significant contribution to Bethel by inviting Bob Hope to come to Memphis stadium for a show. The attendance was disappointing, but the show was very good. Fred became something of a hero. So we all knew that he would be elected, but I stayed in the race anyway. I came in second making me the vice-moderator but I don't think that I was ever called on by Mr. Bryson to do anything but that was just fine with me.

Yet another honor for that year, 1977, Dr. William Odom, the President of Bethel College called and said that the Board of Trustees of Bethel wanted to honor my years in Women's Work by giving me an Honorary Doctorate of Literature. I felt so honored and very undeserving. It was a very special occasion in my life.

I Go to Japan

A few months after I was elected Moderator, I received a letter from my "boss," Dr. Joe Matlock, informing me that a group of people had made contributions that would enable Bill and me to go to Japan! WOW—what a lovely surprise. I couldn't believe it. It so happened that Bill was not able to go, so Beverly Garrett, the new president of the CPW Convention wanted to go in Bill's place and I was delighted to have her. She was an excellent traveling companion. We first went to Japan where, of course, we were treated like royalty! (That is just the way the Japanese are!) Then followed a few days in Hong Kong, and a short trip to mainland China, where, at one time we had Cumberland Presbyterian churches. Unfortunately there was a typhoon in Hong Kong so we had to return by train instead of boat. When we arrived in Hong Kong it was raining so hard that we could hardly see the streets. But we "felt our way" back to our hotel (The Metropole) and arrived safely. When we got back into our room there was a basket of fruit awaiting us with a note of appreciation from the manager.

We had plans go to Beijing from Hong Kong but the Hong Kong people didn't want us to go because of the student uprising on Tiananmen Square. But we had our visas so we went on to Beijing against their better judgment. Fortunately we had a very successful visit and nothing went wrong! Beijing is a beautiful city with a very nice Holiday Inn to accommodate us.

Our tour guides were very knowledgeable and helpful. After a group of visitors left our bus, the tour guides offered to take us by cab to the Square and even got out of the cab to walk with us. The crowd of students had diminished somewhat, but several of them came up to us and asked us to "speak English." We noticed that the sanitary conditions were worsening and it seemed that we saw signs that the group might soon abandon their protest. The following Wednesday, five days later, we watched a local news broadcast show the video of a lone unidentified young man walk out into the streets in an effort to block a column of Chinese military tanks. An end to the student protest against the communist government was in sight.

Bill and I Take Our First Trip after Retirement

The first thing that we did after both of us were "retired" was to plan a month-long trip to somewhere. I let Bill decide because he had traveled so much that I thought that he might like to go somewhere he had never been. So, one day he came in with an itinerary: from Nashville to North Carolina to visit Becky and Ralph Barnes, then up the East coast to Philadelphia, Washington to see Bill's cousin, Col. and Mrs. Thomas St. John, New York to see Tammy St. John, to Connecticut to visit Mark and Jean Clements, some air force friends, and on up into Canada, then back to Owl's Head, Maine to visit Adam and Dorothy (some Montclair friends), and then back to Nashville. I was very happy with his plans and the people that we might get to see on our trip.

One of the highlights of the trip was sitting on the back porch of the Beck's and watching the lobster boats—and having a lobster dinner (all that we could eat!) When we were in Owl's Head, Maine, I had a craving for some cooked vegetables! We went to several restaurants and they all had only a salad with an entrée. We finally found a place that offered to prepare us some "stir fry" vegetables. So we settled for that.

When we got to Knoxville on the last leg of the trip we thought that we could make it home easily, but decided that we would stay there for the last night of our vacation. We checked into a motel and went down the road and there was a Shoney's, so we turned in. Low and behold! They had a Vegetable Bar. That night we had turnip greens, squash, beans, fried okra, and the best fried corn that I had ever eaten! To think that we had driven a couple thousand miles and our best meal was at Shoney's! (At least it seemed that way!) It was good to be at home again—at least for a while.

Our First Grandchild Is Born

Jan and George moved to West Tennessee in 1966. They lived with George's parents (Catherine and Buck) until they could find a place to live. It was during their stay there that Jan learned that she was pregnant. She was so excited because she was anxious to have a baby. Before Catherine and Buck moved back to Arkansas, Jan and George found a two bedroom house for rent in Greenfield, Tennessee not far from McKenzie, the home of Bethel College and a mere 30 minute drive from George's folks in Martin. George was interested in music and electronics. He had a job at a place that manufactured capacitors and also got together a little band, while Jan was busy getting ready for their first child. Jill Suzanne Clinton was born in February 1967, in a hospital in Union City, so, of course I had to drive over to see my first grand-baby. I remember driving down to their home in Greenfield and shopping for some groceries so there would be plenty of food for the new "family." That is what grandparents do!

Jill was a bright star to all of the family. She was the first grandchild and never wanted for attention. Jan had to have surgery at Vanderbilt when Jill was only five months old, so we loved having time on our own with her. During her school years, she liked playing with Barbie dolls, was extremely studious, took piano lessons, and had lots of friends. About age sixteen, Jill moved in with us and attended Glencliff High School and took a retail job near what is still today 100 Oaks Mall. She grew up and there is more about her ahead.

A Second Grandchild

Twelve and a half months after Jill's birth, Jan and George's second child, Jay, was born. William Clinton was born in the same hospital and I was able to be there for the event. She was a very happy mom! Jay was a lively little tow-headed boy. Jill was already walking and wanted to be her momma's little helper. She would go and get a diaper for him when asked.

When their babies were six months and eighteen months George found a job in Memphis. He and Jan, toddler Jill, and baby Jay moved to an apartment there. During their year there George was diagnosed with diabetes. While in the hospital he and Jan learned about the disease and how to treat it with medication, diet and daily shots of insulin. It was a blessing that they discovered the illness and got George into treatment—for life. It didn't seem to interfere with George's business and he continued working in the music recording business.

Some years later Jan and George divorced and parted company. He married again and moved to Nashville where he continued in the music business and had a studio on Music Row in Nashville and was very respected by his peers in the business. Sadly, George developed heart trouble and died in 2011.

What I remember the most about Jay is his childhood in Shreveport. They lived in a very nice neighborhood with many children who enjoyed riding bikes and skateboards. His next door friends, Clay and Trey, were in and out of the house whenever they could be. The boys shared many fun times. Jay was into doing whatever needed to repair his and his friends' skateboards and even set up shop in a dog house in the corner of the backyard complete with tools and even a sign "skateboard repair". He liked fixing things. Even today he enjoys doing renovations and building. He has even built his wife a lovely cherry dresser.

Their neighborhood was very near a large "duck park." On a bike the kids could be there in a flash. Swing sets and other playground equipment kept the children moving and laughing, and they always looked forward to duck feeding times.

After graduation, Jay moved to Nashville to live with Daddy Bill and me; working and enjoying my cooking! At some point he decided to attend Middle Tennessee State University (MTSU) in Murfreesboro. He lived with a couple of guys and eventually set his sights on physical therapy. Jay even got into playing rugby on campus, liked working out and riding his bike.

From MTSU's graduation, he entered the University of Tennessee at Chattanooga and earned a degree in exercise science. After getting established as a personal trainer in

Nashville, Jay continued his hobbies of road and mountain biking, camping, traveling to visit former college buddies and dabbling in photography. He also met Christine Chancey. Over the next couple of years they enjoyed similar interests and the relationship flourished into a permanent union. After falling in love with the Blue Ridge Mountains and beautiful terrain of North Carolina, Jay accepted a job offer in Asheville. Christine followed a few months later where the two set up housekeeping. As of this writing, Christine is using her professional skills in the bursar's office at the campus of South College. They bought a home in a cozy suburb and enjoy their neighbors, flower and vegetable gardening, and home improvement projects. Both Jay and Christine continue to take advantage of what the area has to offer outdoor enthusiasts. They are also parents to their sweet black dog, Hodi, whom we all adore. Though we would love to have them closer, Asheville is a wonderful place for family to visit!

I Purchase a Farm

I had often chided Bill for putting as much as he could every month into Genesco Stock. "Well, what do you think that I should do?" "I think that you should buy a piece of land" was always my response. I suppose my father had instilled that idea into my brain for many years and I was in favor of seeing what we might find to invest in. A few weeks later I was driving down Highway 96 to Manchester, Tennessee for a speaking engagement. There on the road was a large sign that caught my eye:

"CLAYBROOK FARM TO BE SOLD—40
ACRES
WEDNESDAY 11 A.M."

I continued on my journey to Winchester. I had been invited to stay with a lady who had a lovely farm with a view of the pasture from the breakfast table. Now, that really got me in the mood for a farm. (The Claybrook name had significance to me as the property belonged to the family of Fannie Claybrook, our maid from my girls' early years and beyond. Fannie had told me at some point about that farm. She would love for me to buy it and build on it and she would come take care of me the rest of my life). So I arrived home

187

that night, called Bill and told him that I "was going to purchase a 40-acre farm". He was taken aback, but recovered and we had a good conversation. He finally said "You may go but don't spend over $10,000. I went and did as he suggested—almost! I bid $10,500 and got it. After he came home I took him out to see "my farm" and he was very pleased and thought that it was a good buy! I really bought it with the intention of building a home there, but that was not to be. We did enjoy fishing in the pond, picking plums and blackberries, but building a home there became impractical. Bill had developed cancer and was in need of chemotherapy. So, ten years later, I sold the farm. But it was a great investment as I sold it for over $100,000. That money invested has been very good to me since Bill's death in 1993.

Susan Gets Married

By the time Susan had graduated from Furman University in Greeneville, South Carolina, she had decided to get a law degree. She had been looking into law schools and finally decided to attend either Vanderbilt University or Mercer University in Macon, Georgia and made application. Vanderbilt turned her down as they had a quota of ten female law students and the quota had been filled. So, she accepted the opportunity to attend Mercer's Walter F. George School of Law. She excelled in her studies and enjoyed all of her years there. However, in her second year she met a young man and called us to announce that she was in love! We were excited and asked a few questions:

What does he look like? "He's over six feet tall, has black curly hair, and is a fine southern gentleman—and he loves me!"

How did you meet? "He was a good friend of a student that I was dating."

Is he a student? "No, he was at one time but joined the army and was in Russia as a translator for several years, returned with the intention of attending Mercer and pursue a degree in Russian, but the school had dropped the course, so he got a job."

"Well, what does he do? "He manages a liquor store."
"What will I tell your grandmother? "Tell her that he manages

a liquor store!" So I did. Her response: "Well, as long as our society needs liquor stores, then it is an honorable job!" I was relieved! (Our mother was a pretty realistic person!)

In June, Susan and Frank came for a visit and plans began for their wedding. We decided to have it on Sunday afternoon, September 9, 1969. It was our first time to meet Frank even though we had talked on the phone and he asked Bill and me if we would allow him to become a member of our family. Indeed, he was a big man, very nice looking and had good manners just like Susan had said. There again, we were relieved.

It was fun shopping for a wedding dress and we found one that was "just right" for her petite statue. She had asked Jan, her roommate Emily Lawyer, and another law school friend by the name of Karen. It was to be a Sunday afternoon affair at Brookhaven Church, and our pastor, Vernon Burrow, would have the service. Frank's father, Bill and Bill's brother were to be the best men. We were pleased that some members of Frank's family would be able to attend: Frank's parents, Louise and Frank Steger, his aunt Edna Steger, and his greataunt Margaret.

Two months later, everyone came in on Thursday morning—two days before the wedding. We had a rehearsal party in a private room at the Holiday Inn in Franklin on Saturday night that was hosted by Frank's parents and Aunt Edna. It was a lovely affair and we had a great time. On

Sunday we all went to church and had communion together. Three hours later was the wedding and it went off with only one hitch: the photographer didn't show up! But Jay St. John made some slides, and the caterer's son made a few black and white snapshots for us, so we were not completely bereft of pictures for the memory book.

For the next 40 years Macon, Georgia was home for Susan and Frank and they were very happy. They rented an apartment not too far from school and work. It served them well for a while but they began hankering for a home and found one near the place where they were living and moved in one happy day—a home that they were to spend the rest of their lives in. Susan continued to go to Law School there and graduated a year later. Jay and Remley, Mother, and Bill and I were able to be there for the special event. Frank's parents and Edna were there as well. The interesting thing is that Susan and Frank planned and prepared the "graduation dinner" at their apartment. How well I remember Frank coming into the living room where we were all seated, and graciously carrying a silver tray with wild rice and baked Cornish hens. That was followed by a tray with a bowl of green beans, and a large salad. For dessert they served ice cream with fresh peaches laced with almonds. They were so happy and very proud of that meal that they prepared and served together.

Now the time had come for Susan to find a job. She

went to many law firms with her credentials but no one seemed inclined to employ a woman. But she persisted and after several months she succeeded and the newspapers acknowledged her success by putting several articles about her in their papers with pictures. Her dream had finally come true!

Not long after her graduation, Frank's parents decided to move to Florida—something that they had planned to do after Frank, Sr. retired. Susan and Frank were disappointed but honored their desires and bid them "farewell." Frank, Sr.'s sister, Edna stayed in Macon where she worked as a librarian until the time of her retirement. She was very good to Susan and Frank and they were very good to her. In fact, when her health declined she chose to go into a nursing home and Susan saw to her every need during her days there until the time of her death.

Susan's career as a lawyer continued for the rest of her life. One of her greatest achievements was the establishment of a facility for abused women and children. For the first few years that project was her major focus. She received the support of the doctors and lawyers and the judicial system as well as some abused women in locating a site for the facility. She also informed the public of its important role in the lives of women in the area. Frank continued to work at the liquor store for two years and then worked in a bookstore for a couple of years. He later took the Civil Service Exam and began working for the Post Office and worked there for the rest of his life.

Frank became a sober alcoholic in 1993, and immediately became an active member of AA and continued as an active member and leader for the rest of his life. He never missed a meeting—even when he was on vacation. I really admired him for that.

Our First Great Grandchild, Chelsea

In the meantime, our granddaughter, Jill, met Robert Lee Owens who was well-intentioned but an immature young man. They married and rented a trailer home and were excited over the promise of a child who was born at Vanderbilt hospital on January 11, 1986. They named her Chelsea Suzanne Catherine. She was adorable and we were all in love with her. One morning I called to check on Jill and she didn't answer. With a new child, I began to worry, so I went over to her home and no one was there. I stayed parked by the trailer until Jill drove up, smiling and happy—she had gotten a job delivering papers and had taken the baby with her. I tell that story because it illustrates just how ingenious and responsible Jill was and still is. She could always get a job, and at the same time take good care of her children.

It wasn't long before they found an apartment between Harding Place and Murfreesboro Pike—and not very far from us. We enjoyed an occasional visit with Chelsea—a darling, bright, and beautiful child whom "Daddy Bill" and I adored! The time came when Chelsea's dad couldn't deal with the responsibilities of parenthood and he and Jill parted company. Jill worked and was able to enroll Chelsea into our church's daycare. They came to services at Brookhaven Church and Jill presented Chelsea for baptism at nine months of age.

Time passed by and we learned that Jill, having not remarried, met and became a friend with Bob Weisz from Sarasota, Florida. Bob offered to take her to Sarasota so his mother could help her and Chelsea find a place to live. Jill called us and asked, "Will that be all right?" Bill and I were flattered that she sought our opinions. It turned out to be a good decision. She liked Sarasota and so did four year old Chelsea. Bob and his mother were very helpful in finding a safe place for them to live and life was good again.

As has been mentioned, Jill has always been self-sufficient. She found work soon after the move to Sarasota. She and Chelsea were able to move into a duplex and enjoyed discovering new friends and their new city. Chelsea had many fun experiences and, after entering school, proved to be a good student. She participated in the field day programs, coordinated neighborhood plays, went often to the local library, and learned how to do crafty things with her mom. "Daddy Bill" and I were always glad to have her visit us in Nashville. Traveling via airplane to see us got to be a very comfortable mode of transportation for her.

At age ten things changed for Chelsea when she was diagnosed with heart disease. Jill made sure she had the best of doctors and care. She kept life as normal as possible, even during and beyond Chelsea's heart transplant at age fourteen. I was even able to fulfill her dream and take her to Japan to stay in the home of Masaharu and Kaye Asayama, whom

Chelsea met one summer at my home. She met so many caring adults and youth of the local church, toured, and experienced special Japanese customs. It was a memorable ten days and all went well.

As Chelsea continued in school, she enjoyed her friends, got very comfortable with computer technology, read, did crafts, and still flew to see her Nashville family and her church family. She was crowned "Queen" at a high school event and as many in the family that could, attended her graduation. There were more challenges and physical insults to her daughter but Jill helped Chelsea become a college freshman and complete two subjects, later receiving an honors award.

The loving commitment of Chelsea's parents and sister, along with the medical community, and Hospice care for her at home were incredible. Over time her body weakened and at age twenty-one, she made the decision to take medicine only for pain relief. Jan and I went down to Sarasota to be with her and her devoted family. Those were painful but very sweet last days for all of us. Chelsea was awake off and on and we got to talk, watch TV, and tell stories from time to time. I asked her one day to tell me her favorite Bible character. I wanted to have a painting or statue to put into the Children's library at the church in her memory. She thought for a moment and said, "I think that Rahab was a gutsy lady." I have found a picture and am in the process of having it framed. Chelsea herself demonstrated amazing strength. We will always be grateful for the expressions over the years of love and attention to her and her family from our local church and throughout the denomination. Our own pastor, Kip Rush, flew down to deliver comforting care and made a lasting impression.

In May, 2007, many gathered at Brenthaven Cumberland Presbyterian Church in Brentwood, Tennessee to have a memorial service for Chelsea, remembering her thoughtfulness, spunk, spirit, and bravery. Rev. John Leggett, who had baptized Chelsea at age 12, delivered the sermon and I was able to share a eulogy. We all still miss that beautiful young girl but when you see a butterfly, remember the new life that Chelsea will have forever.

A Little Sister for Chelsea and Another Great Granddaughter, Rachel

Jill's and Bob's friendship blossomed into marriage and the birth of a little sister for Chelsea. It was Halloween 1994. Chelsea was eight and a half and excited about trick or treating! Jill was having signals that their second child was about to arrive so Jill asked a friend to watch Chelsea so the expectant parents could get to the hospital. Rachel Eleanor was born the next morning!! Rachel added lots of joy for all of us and still does!!

The two sisters grew very close. Their neighborhood was full of children—they played games, put on plays, celebrated holidays, had sleep overs, trips to the library, parks and beach—the list goes on. Jill made sure her two girls had fun through learning, laughter, and lots of love.

Since I have an art background, I was hopeful when Rachel showed early signs of having a flare for drawing, but as time went on that interest waned. Rachel had other interests. She loved swinging in the backyard while singing songs, riding her tricycle and playing with the big kids. Rachel always was and still is a top student and enjoys learning. As they grew, she and Chelsea stayed close and shared many activities together and with their neighborhood buddies. Both of Jill's girls loved to entertain an audience.

As a growing girl, Rachel has certainly provided the family with some special memories. Jan told me that one time, when Rachel was not even three years old, the two of them were in the backyard of their Sarasota home and Rachel wanted to swing. As she did, Rachel sang every word of "I've been working on the railroad". For her first few years Rachel chattered a lot. She knew what she was saying, and her mom and sister could decipher it and by the time she was three or four we could all understand her well. She had her own language going on in that very smart brain! She loved going to pre-school at the Berry Patch and the teachers and other children loved Rachel back. As was pointed out earlier she tried and succeeded at times keeping up with the bigger children in the neighborhood—like learning to ride a bicycle and a favorite of hers, a razor scooter. One thing that is interesting about her is that not only did she like to play but after their meals she liked the chore of taking a paper towel and Windex and cleaning the glass top of their kitchen table! In elementary school she excelled in all subjects, keeping the teachers on their toes. She was published in one of the school papers that spoke to her kindness and character.

Rachel continued to be a really good student and made sweet elementary and middle school friends and just plain had fun. After moving to Nashville in 2008, she adapted well to the eighth grade for the one year she attended J.T. Moore. High school changes brought its challenges, but her desire to learn was her priority and she graduated with honors and also college credits.

The summer before her senior year, her maternal grandmother (Jan) took her to New York! They saw the sights, the crowds, stood in Times Square, witnessed the hustle and bustle of downtown among a few things. Jan had not been there herself since she was about nine years old, when we lived for a year in New Jersey and took our two girls to the "Big Apple". According to Jan, she and Rachel would never have gotten anywhere if it wasn't for Rachel's keen sense of direction and great mind!! They included staying part of their nine days there in Saugerties, New York, about two hours north of Manhattan. That is where cousin Kathy Stevens lives and owns CAS-the Catskill Animal Sanctuary, a refuge for abused and abandoned farm animals. It was a hands-on learning experience that neither one of them will forget.

Vacations in Florida

In the summer of 1981, the family was on vacation at Silver Dunes in Destin, Florida. On one of our nights there, we took a stroll down the beach and a young man gave Bill a flyer inviting us to attend an open house at one of the motels on the beach. Much to my surprise Bill decided to look into it. I suppose the salesperson was an expert, or we really liked the place, but we found ourselves plunking down some money on a one-bedroom unit! It turned out to be a good idea and we have spent many years going to Destin in September and loving every minute! One year there was a bad storm that decimated the town and especially the beach. So we were told not to come. We were very disappointed. Weather has interfered with only a handful of our trips there in these last 30+ years. After Bill's death in 1993, I bought another condo in the same resort so more members could enjoy the beach together. We have met a lot of nice people who had the same experience and loved the place as much as we have. I hope it will carry on through the years to come giving our family a great place to reunite each year on the beautiful Emerald Coast.

My Son-in-law

I cannot complete my musings without including the man in Jan's life who has enhanced all of us. Jan and Larry were introduced by his niece, a co-worker of Jan's at the hospital. They met on a blind date in September 2003 while my friend Rose and I were in Destin at our condo. The very next weekend he arrived at our church and the two of us got to meet. The rest is history. They announced their engagement around Valentine's Day at a family meal and married at Brookhaven Cumberland Presbyterian Church in July 2004. He loves to vegetable garden so for their wedding gift I gave them a tiller!!! He has used it at least twice a year to grow both summer and winter vegetables and we have all enjoyed the harvests. They have fun times, share worship and work well together. He is a dear "other son" and I'm so glad.

Our Fiftieth Anniversary

We celebrated our 50th Wedding Anniversary on July 30, 1992. It was at Brookhaven Church. We had a glorious time seeing friends from everywhere! There were over 200 people who joined us for the event. All of the family were here including Susan and Frank, Jan, Jill, Jay, and Chelsea who was all dressed up in an organdy dress (and added some of my dangling pearl earrings) and helped us to greet our friends. Maureen Dement made a beautiful cake and we served punch to go with it.

Bill had been undergoing chemotherapy for cancer off and on for several years. He seemed a bit weak but was his usual gracious self. As soon as the party was over he went home and on to bed. That wasn't good news. So, on Monday we went back to St. Thomas Hospital and under the care of the doctors again. Things were up and down for six months and we were fully aware that the end was near. He was a valiant patient and continued to cooperate with the doctors' instructions. Our grandson, Jay, was living with us and going to college at Middle Tennessee University in Murfreesboro. Hospice supplied us with a hospital bed for Bill so he could be as comfortable as possible, as well as other equipment we would need for his care. A nurse would come periodically to evaluate needs, not only for Bill but for me. By early January his condition had worsened. I went into the room, took his hand and asked him if he wanted anything. He said "No thank you… but I would like a prayer." I responded "do you want to pray or do you want me to pray?" He whispered "I want to." Bill prayed "Dear God, I am going on a long trip. Please take care of my family while I am away." I began to sing his favorite hymn: "Lord, We Are Able" and he joined in with a few words. At some point during his last days, Susan had arrived to be with her daddy. Jay, Jill and Chelsea visited when they could to see "Daddy Bill." What a memorable and blessed ending for a wonderful man's life.

After Bill's death, I took on a project that I hadn't thought of until I became a member of the Theology and Social Concerns Committee of Nashville Presbytery. When I first met with the committee I asked them if they had any social ministries that they were working on and the reply was "No—we haven't thought of anything. We were hoping that you might have some ideas." "As a matter of fact I do. I have been thinking that Nashville Presbytery might be interested in building a Habitat House." "Well, how do we do that?" "I don't know but I will find out."

So the following week I called the Habitat Office and told them what I wanted. They immediately gave me the name of Rick Beech, who was the Middle Tennessee Area HFH Director. I called Rick and asked him to meet with the committee so we could formulate a recommendation to give to the Presbytery at the next meeting.

Our committee made the recommendation that "Nashville Presbytery consider building a house in cooperation with Habitat for Humanity." We had Rick Beech at the meeting to answer all of the questions that anyone might have. After a lengthy discussion, the Presbytery voted to build their first House for and with Habitat for Humanity. That was a giant step.

We relied on Habitat for Humanity to find a good location and they found a lot in the Clarksville community that was convenient to the members of Nashville Presbytery. The recipient family put many hours of "sweat equity" as required by HFH and were very grateful and deserving. The people in the presbytery volunteered by the dozens and the home was dedicated in the spring of about 1993. In fact, Nashville Presbytery voted unanimously to put $10,000 a year into the budget and build one every year. As far as I know they have continued their building projects. (At this writing in 2013 the Presbytery is still building a Habitat House every year).

A year later, Michael Sharpe, at the Denominational Center, invited me to be the Denominational Coordinator for HFH and I accepted. My job was to encourage other presbyteries in the denomination to check into the possibility of working with HFH and try to build some houses. That didn't work out very well as most of the presbyteries of the denomination are too "spread out" to take on such a project. So my job ended after three years.

Some Special Guests

One night my phone rang and a friend, who was the executive for Church Women United (National) was on the line with a request: would I please find homes for ten women who were coming to Nashville for a bit of rest before going to Scarritt-Bennett Center for another meeting. I told her that I would see what I could do. Within an hour or so I had found places for seven women but didn't know what I would do with the other three. Even though I was going to be out of town on Friday afternoon until Saturday noon, I decided to let them stay in my home. I met them at the airport, directed the other ladies to their hostess who were awaiting them, and then I brought my three home with me. It was very late so I sent them to bed as I knew that they were very tired. I told them that I would awaken them at 7:00 a.m. and we would have breakfast at 8:00 a.m.

Friday morning I prepared a "southern" breakfast of biscuits, sausage, eggs and grits and called them to the table. After we sat down, I told them that I needed to have a bit of time for getting acquainted. The lady to my left was Lucy Kasicenda from Uganda. The person across from me was Una Matthews from Guyana in South America. She was a United Methodist. The lady to my right was Mona Wong from Singapore, and an Episcopalian. I suddenly realized that around my little breakfast table were four continents, four denominations, four nationalities, and four races! So, we had a prayer and sang "In Christ there is No East or West." I will never forget the joy of that occasion!

I Become the First Woman Moderator

I really don't remember who initiated the idea for me to be the moderator of General Assembly for the year 1988. But, I accepted having no idea with who I might be in contention. But, it turned out there were no other nominees. This meant unless someone was nominated from the floor I would be the new moderator. That was a formidable challenge for me. Even though I had traveled all over the denomination, knew a lot of people and had committed to a number of roles in the life of the Cumberland Presbyterian Church, I was still in awe of the possibility! I was somewhat afraid as well. E.G. Sims was the delegate from Nashville Presbytery so he made the "nomination speech" and I was elected. I appointed E.G. to be the parliamentarian and managed to get through the meeting! It was then my responsibility to visit churches and presbyteries during the year and represent the denomination at several meetings. It was a very interesting year.

Another Honorary Degree

Yet another surprise came when I received a letter from Dr. Jay Earheart-Brown, President of Memphis Theological Seminary, telling me that the Board of Trustees had unanimously voted to give me an Honorary Doctor of Divinity Degree at the next graduation ceremony to be held May 10, 2008. I was floored! And I could not believe it. Of course I accepted the honor and Jan, along with my friend Pam Barnett, came to Memphis to help me celebrate. The sanctuary of the church where the graduation ceremony was held seemed "awesome" to me and I really felt so unworthy. But I wore a robe that they gave me and after the "event" I was draped with a beautiful stole. I will probably never have an occasion to wear it but it will be in the family as a symbol of that special event.

Susan and Frank

Susan and Frank usually joined us in Destin in September. We had a family reunion every year after Bill's death in 1993. In September of that year, I purchased another unit so I could will each of our daughters a unit with the awareness that they would be able to see each other at least once a year! And we did for a while but Susan died quite suddenly in May 2009. A mother is not supposed to outlive her children!

Susan had been to court the morning of May 2009, then to the store and home. When Frank came home from his afternoon meeting, he would see Susan and prepare for work. That day he noticed her sleeping soundly in their bed, so he did not disturb her and left for the post office. When he returned at midnight, he found her lifeless on the bed.

Three months after Susan's death Frank died. His death was just as unexpected as Susan's. It seems that he was to have breakfast with a group of friends at 8:00 a.m. on Sunday morning and when he didn't show up, one person told the group that he had a key to the house. They all went to the house and he was on the floor by the bed in which Susan had died. Jan and I went down immediately and stayed until we had taken care of the necessary business—for Susan as well as Frank. The months following were filled with Jan making many trips to Macon, and it was a very difficult assignment for her—both in time and emotions.

Both of their memorial services were held at St. Paul's Episcopal Church in Macon where they had been members for many years. I did a eulogy for each of them and am so glad that I was able to do that little service for them. I had told the attendees that they really knew Susan better than I did! She had lived in Macon for 40 years and had left home for school (college and graduate school) at the age of eighteen. (Susan willed Brenthaven Church in Brentwood and St. Paul's Church in Macon $10,000 each for which I am very grateful).

Several family members (Jill, Dwayne, Rachel, Jay, Christine and my niece, Beverly Ann) were able to be with us and that was good and helpful.

A Move to Nashville-near Family

One year after Chelsea's death, Jill, Rachel, and Dwayne moved to Nashville and we were delighted. They stayed here with us for some months and it was good to have them around—a good reunion! The first Sunday they were here they chose to look for a church with "contemporary" worship and they did. However, the next Sunday they decided to attend church with me at Brenthaven. They continued and soon joined Brenthaven—that made me very happy to be able to see them every Sunday. They have continued to be very active by being greeters, helping cook for special events and teaching in the children's department.

Following their move to Nashville, Rachel started to middle school at John Trotwood Moore in the eighth grade and then transferred to Hillsboro High School. She took advanced classes and some in the International Baccalaureate program they offered and did very well. To enhance her learning she did her final year in Middle College High School at Nashville State where after just the first semester she had her credits to graduate plus received a number of college credits to put her a few steps ahead. A pretty mature young lady, Rachel wanted to make her own money so while in school so she worked at a nearby restaurant. After inquiring into several colleges and a couple of road trips, she chose to attend the University of North Carolina in Asheville. I have no idea what her major will be but I am sure that she will do well in whatever she pursues. An added bonus: she is in school very near her Uncle Jay and Aunt Christine. She lives in the dorm this first year and may later go to live with Jay and Christine. They have mentioned making a little apartment for her in their spacious basement. Time will tell.

After the family moved here in 2008, Jill and Dwayne both found employment fairly quickly. Jill got an office job in the physical therapy clinic at Baptist Hospital in Nashville and was made office manager within six months. She is also taking classes in Nursing with a goal of become a nurse (her mom worked as an RN for 34 years). Jill is a precious granddaughter, an asset to her job, our family and a wonderful human being. Likewise, Dwayne works for Continental Machinery Movers and loves his work repairing and driving all kinds of heavy equipment. His job takes him into many different business situations and places and he enjoys sharing his experiences. He is an amazing young man who can "fix" and/or build almost anything. We enjoy having a man in the family who is so talented and handy to have around.

I Am Getting Old

It is the winter of 2014, and I am still dealing with chronic pain from falls that I have had beginning in 2011. I have a lot of back pain, am having therapy and on medications that don't always work. My body is disintegrating but my mind is okay (I think!) I am able to attend church pretty regularly, enjoy my Sunday school class and the worship services at Brenthaven Cumberland Presbyterian Church.

I am grateful to be part of a congregation that supported our pastor taking a well deserved sabbatical. Kip Rush had been with Brenthaven Church for over seven years and it was time. Even so, he chose to wait until his oldest daughter graduated high school so he could include his wife, Jodi, and their two girls or the trip. A few of our members teamed together to write a grant and present it to the Lilly Foundation to financially support all aspects of the sabbatical. Kip was awarded the grant and in the summer of 2013, Kip began a three month journey, and included his family from time to time. It was a working grant and he was required to present a paper to the Foundation upon completion of his time away. Our congregation was also to work together on our dreams and visions for Brenthaven Church. An appointed team made plans and during the summer while our pastor was away we fellowshipped, prayed, dreamed and shared our hopes for the future. We had a number of wonderful ministers and others to fill the pulpit on Sundays and the spirit stayed strong. Upon his return, we celebrated with a great occasion of hugs and blessings and smiles all over the place. It was not only a time of joy but of renewal and resolve to be a better congregation than ever!

Postlude

As I conclude this biography, I can look back over 95 years of a journey filled with joy in abundance, a horde of caring friends, a large number of supportive family members, and a plethora of wonderful memories and experiences too many to count. But, most of all, I am surrounded by Christian people of all colors and races and nations. Who could ask for more than that? And, to add a bit more: I have had the blessing of a "special male friend" who has given me a new understanding of love in later life that I cannot describe—a love that includes friendship, courtship, hugs from afar, and laughter that has no end! Yes, you never get too old to fall in love. And THAT is the biggest surprise of all! Because of our ages, and the distance between us there can be no more, but our "special" friendship abounds with all kinds of emotions—especially joy!

Indeed—I have had the "best life that anyone could possibly have"—a life that has had Jesus Christ at the center. I have loved the Cumberland Presbyterian Church since I first heard of her from the stories I was told by my friend's mother when I was a teenager. The journey has been a very interesting one with many kind and helpful people. A young Cumberland Presbyterian, Matthew Gore, is even printing this manuscript of memories for me. I am grateful for him as well as for the Cumberland Presbyterian Church for the many opportunities of service and joy that she has provided me through the years.

With a heart filled with love and gratitude,

Beverly P. St. John

Family History

For my family now and family to come I want to conclude by sharing some early history that I found in an old Bible that belonged to my father's Aunt Janie. She, in turn had given it to her brother, Ernest, because she felt that he should have it, not only because he was oldest of three sons in the family, but because she knew that Ernest's wife (my mother) was very interested in family history whereas Aunt Janie's other siblings were not.

Paternal Ancestors
(hand written in cursive in an Old Family Bible)

Marriages

George Pickup and Martha Oldham (daughter of William and Martha Oldham)) were married on the 25th of December in 1853 in Staley-wood Church near Lincolnshire, England.

Mr. James M. Capley married Miss Mary Jane Pickup the 5th day of January in 1888 at the residence of J. C. Pettus and wife in Franklin County, Tennessee. Squire Boling officiated

Births

George Pickup was born in the year of our Lord 1828 on the 29th day of August in Backup Derbyshire, England. He died at five minutes to one in the morning of April 20, 1918.

Martha (Oldham) Pickup was born in the year of our Lord 1829 the 2nd day of February in Newton Moore Cheshire, England. She died July 27, 1915 at half past four in the morning.

William Oldham born on April 14, 1800
Martha Oldham born May 29, 1802
Following are children's names:
Mary Ann September 6, 1819
Alice January 3, 1822
Alexander May 20, 1824
James September 13, 1826
Martha February 2, 1829
Twins Thomas and Joseph April 21, 1831
Samuel March 28, 1833
Sophia May 23, 1836
Bettie August 24, 1838
William April 22, 1843
Thomas April 11, 1845

John Capley died August 1, 1876 and wife Rebecca Capley died September 2, 1901. There are no dates of birth found.

Their son **James M. Capley** *was born in 1849 the 20th day of September in Bedford County, near Shelbyville, Tennessee. He died on July 15, 1903 at age 54.*

Mary J. Capley *was born in 1857 in Newton Moore, Cheshire, England*

$$\oplus$$

My father, **Ernest Alexander Pickup** *the son of* **George Alexander** *and* **Martha Pickup** *was born on April 10, 1887 in Shelbyville, Tennessee (died 1970-Nashville Tennessee)*

My mother, **Bessie James Wickware**, *the daughter of* **Evalina Gammon** *and* **Jerry Wickware** *was born on January 7, 1890 in Mitchellville, Tennessee(died 1973).*

Bessie James Wickware *had one sister,* **Velma Gillman Wickware**, *who married* **James Clifton Owen** *in 1929. They had one daughter,* **Judith Gilman Owen** *who was born August, 1932.*

Bessie James Wickware *married* **Ernest Alexander Pickup**

*in June of 1912. They had two children, **Eleanor Ann** (December 26, 1915) and **Beverly Head** born on October 14, 1918.*

29746443R00142

Made in the USA
Charleston, SC
21 May 2014